Pete Nelson

New TREEHOUSES
of the WORLD

ABRADALE, NEW YORK

INTRODUCTION

Treehouses have something to say. They speak in an ancient language, and the message is universal: Climb up and be in harmony with nature. Let go of earthbound encumbrances and be free.

Isn't that a beautiful and relevant message for our world today?

Treehouses possess a transformative power: As soon as you climb through the threshold of a treehouse, you're a changed person. Being held up by the trunk and branches of a tree, surrounded by the raw energy of nature, the soul is inevitably rejuvenated and the spirit lifted.

What if all the important meetings between world leaders were held in treehouses? Something tells me that an awful lot of conflict would be avoided.

The good news is that treehouses continue to gain popularity not only in the United States but also around the world. Many of us are spending more and more time looking inward, and as we do, we are looking upward. Through the tremendous work of people like Richard Louv and his Leave No Child Inside movement, the importance of connecting kids with nature is not only being accepted but it is also being wholeheartedly embraced by our educators. And kids aren't the only ones who need contact with nature—it's necessary for people of all ages. We never grow out of a need for nature.

Last year our company, TreeHouse Workshop, Inc., had the privilege of building two treehouses at one of the most outstanding horticultural centers in the world—Longwood Gardens in Kennett Square, Pennsylvania—in celebration of Arbor Day. Our friends at Forever Young Treehouses (page 90) also built a universally accessible treehouse. When the gates opened, the response was overwhelming. People from all walks of life and all ages swarmed the treehouses, and Longwood Gardens had one of their busiest weekends in memory. Watching the beaming faces of the first wave of visiting children, my heart nearly burst with joy: All of these people had come to experience these treehouses, which put them, whether consciously or not, directly into the arms of nature.

This book aims to inspire. While many of the projects depicted in these pages are complex, I believe that each was built with the same joyful spirit. I am humbled and excited by the ever-growing body of work that kind people regularly share with me. I must also confess a noticeable bias toward a celebration of the work of our loyal and creative associates and employees. Jake Jacob, my partner in TreeHouse Workshop, Inc., for over twelve years now, has consistently produced a product well beyond anyone's expectations, including my own. So please, enter into these pages with a happy heart and a hope to leave your earthbound life behind, if only for a little while.

Bird House **(above)** and Canopy Cathedral **(opposite)**, two treehouses designed and built by TreeHouse Workshop at Longwood Gardens in Pennsylvania.

CHAPTER 1
The Journey

My daughter Emily was thirteen when she decided that our pretty town of Fall City, Washington, was too small for her taste. Even at that tender age Emily carried a lot of weight in the family. It was late in the winter of 2004 and within two days she had my wife, Judy, and I committed to spending the next school year in Barcelona, Spain. Her younger brothers, Charlie and Henry, were not enthused, but Judy and I decided it was the perfect opportunity to shake things up a bit and to travel, two things I love to do, and we were sure it would benefit the entire family. We ended up smack-dab in the middle of Barcelona, a city I knew nothing about, but at the age of forty-two, I was about to have what would turn out to be the best year of my life (so far).

I tell this story because, at this midpoint in my life, I was presented with a unique opportunity to take stock and think about what I wanted to do in the second half of my life. When I left for Spain, the company I cofounded—TreeHouse Workshop, Inc.—was taking up only about half of my time; I spent the rest of it building regular houses in Seattle. This had been going on for more than twelve years. My partner at TreeHouse Workshop, Jake Jacob, and office manager Anna Daeuble, who had been at it full time, were the ones building the company. We also had four full-time carpenters. I had a hard time believing that we could make it work, but we were proving that a market for treehouses actually did exist.

Yet here I was in Barcelona, wondering what I would do when I got home. By this time, I had been blessed (for better or worse) with the moniker "the treehouse guy." So why was I holding back? Part of the answer came with the advice of a new friend. John Allenberg was in Barcelona doing the exact same thing with his family that we were doing with ours. He and I met early in our year there at a school function, and with our shared interests in live music and mountain biking, we became fast friends. During one of our daily explorations of the city and of ourselves, John reminded me that, in any endeavor, where there is a will, there's a way. I responded that supporting a family of five on a treehouse builder's salary was a scary prospect. "So boost your rates," he suggested with a shrug. Sometimes the obvious escapes me.

I soon found my passion growing for the notion that treehouses could be used for the greater good. Wouldn't it be wonderful to get more people to experience treehouses, to get more people inspired to go out in the backyard with their children and friends and make a little magic happen? I am moved by the work of Bill Allen and his Forever Young organization, which builds universally accessible treehouses. My friend Taka in Japan is raising environmental awareness by building treehouses in his country. As our time in Spain went by, it began to dawn on me that I wanted to be around all of this and be a part of it on a full-time basis.

As our year of not building treehouses in Spain started to wind down, I was seized with the overwhelming desire to build a treehouse in Turo Park, a five-acre manicured oasis directly across the street from our apartment where I had spent time sipping *claras* (a delicious beer and lemonade combo), reading books, and playing with the kids. I had also spent a lot of time in the park attempting landscape paintings, the canvases for which were beautiful doors that I had salvaged from the remodeling and

During my year off in Barcelona, I discovered I was not cut out to be an oil painter. However, my canvases made of old doors became great treehouse building materials.

renovation jobs going on all around us in the city. In fact, my pack-rat ways were starting to overwhelm our small apartment. The things you find in the construction dumpsters of a storied city like Barcelona are amazing! What began as a collection of "canvases" and architectural artifacts became the shabby-chic decor of our sparsely adorned home. It took me a while, but I finally realized that I was subconsciously assembling a treehouse, just waiting to be acknowledged and brought into the light of day. What a great way to clean out the apartment! But I also wanted to leave a small gift behind for my new Catalonian friends. A perfect oak tree beckoned from the park.

A permit for such an endeavor did not quite fit the spirit of the plan, which was to create something that seemed to have sprung up naturally and organically on its own, so it was decided that the assembly would occur in the middle of the night over a noisy holiday weekend in June. My friend John had by this time hit the roads of Europe for a family adventure so I recruited another able-bodied expat named Justin to help me make it happen. The installation went off without a hitch. We did the preassembly in

I have many favorite trees at Tree-house Point, but the one that captures the essence of this beautiful property is a broadleaf maple that spiders its mossy limbs over the salmon-bearing Raging River.

the apartment and tossed everything over the perimeter fence when it was time to build. Wood salvaged from a neighboring building provided the base of the platforms while doors and mouldings provided most of the rest of the structure. We worked while holiday pyrotechnic explosions burst in the sky above us, so not a soul interrupted or impeded our progress. We finished at sunrise.

The next morning Justin and I sat in our aerie on the frames of some beautiful old chairs, sipping from a pitcher of hastily made mojitos, and watching the dogwalkers file in through the gates. Being semi camouflaged twenty feet up, they couldn't see us, but we surely could see them. As the sun filtered over and through the surrounding buildings, and the rum and exhaustion started to settle into our bones, we felt like we were transported to another plane of consciousness. No one noticed us for some time, until finally, the treehouse was spotted. People were thrilled by it. Sadly, the park manager failed to see the magic in it, and though official action often takes months to kick into gear in Spain, this guy proved another side of "where there's a will, there's a way": He had the treehouse removed early on the very first day after the holidays. It had lasted all of three days.

After this incident, it became clear to me that treehouses were to dominate the next phase of my life. Upon my return, I discovered that Jake, Anna, and carpenter Joel "Bubba" Smith of TreeHouse Workshop had collaborated brilliantly on Heidi's Treehouse (page 30). Clearly, the company had survived my long absence. I then told them about my desire to commit myself full time to the business of building treehouses and together we made a pact to take the company to the next level and make it thrive on a much larger scale. We decided to schedule a major treehouse-building workshop, our third, and it filled almost instantly. As John Allenberg had suggested in Barcelona, we boosted our rates. And people kept calling.

A few months after my return, I received what I could only interpret as a sign from the heavens. This sign appeared in the form of a "for sale" sign by the side of a main drag heading into Seattle. When I stopped my truck to have a look, I discovered a primordial forest that stretched from the road down to the spectacular Raging River. Within minutes of entering that forest, any lingering doubts I may have had about the direction that my life was going to take melted away. The next phase would involve nature, education, and, most of all, treehouses. And I could hardly believe the good luck at finding this bit of land. That one-acre piece turned out to be the middle slice in a pie that became almost four acres and the beginnings of a dream retreat that we now call Treehouse Point.

Three years later, Treehouse Point is home to the Northwest Treehouse School, the annual Global Treehouse Symposium held in September, and at this time three well-appointed treehouses that offer overnight accommodations. There is a main lodge that sits firmly on the ground where we can feed up to forty people, as well as a separate building where gatherings of all kinds can occur. As we navigate the tricky development rules of King County, Washington, our hope is to build as many as ten treehouses and also to work with King County officials to develop guidelines that demonstrate how to build treehouses responsibly in sensitive environments.

In chapter 3 we will take a close look at the first treehouse to be built at Treehouse Point, called the Temple of the Blue Moon. But first let's take a look at the current technology connecting treehouses to trees in ways that make treehouse living safe for everyone, trees included.

The Northwest Treehouse School is based at Treehouse Point. Along with teaching all aspects of responsible treehouse building, the school fosters a working relationship between treehouse builders and building officials. A goal of the school is to help develop an open standard that will one day be recognized in the International Building Code.

CHAPTER 2
State-of-the-Art Treehouse Technology

We all know that anybody in their right mind likes treehouses, but do trees like treehouses? Indeed, they do. In fact, the more we learn about how trees react to fasteners and the weight of a treehouse, the more we like what we see.

The key to keeping a tree healthy and happy when building a treehouse is to make each connection count. Peppering a tree with nails creates weak connections and can stress the tree while it heals multiple wounds. Larger and fewer fasteners are what the tree calls for and, while size can vary, the idea is to limit the number of penetrations into the tree.

A major advancement in tree-fastening technology came in 1997 with the introduction of an attachment device, an artificial limb for lack of a better word, that arborist and builder Jonathan Fairoaks brought to the annual World Treehouse Association Conference in Takilma, Oregon. It was a three-inch diameter stainless-steel pin that, when sunk into the heartwood of a tree, was able to support far more weight than anything we had attempted thus far. The simple device caught the attention of Michael Garnier, host of the conference and renowned treehouse hotelier, who, for eight years, had been fighting with Josephine County in Oregon to get his treehouses approved. Michael had been searching for a measurable fastening solution that would satisfy his local building codes, so a large part of the early conferences, which began in 1996, revolved around efforts to destroy anything that we could bolt into a tree. Over the course of the next year, and with the help of his head engineer/guru Charley Greenwood, Michael refined a tree-bolt design that came to be known as the Garnier Limb, or GL.

Above: Richard checks the level as a GL with a five-inch boss (the fat part) is twisted into the tree. The bolts should be as level as possible. **Right:** Michael Garnier sells many GLs like the powder-coated gray ones pictured. Trees in the northwest grow surprisingly quickly, so I prefer a GL with a longer stem, the part of the GL that sticks out from the tree (like the stainless-steel version pictured). While trees grow taller only at their tips, they grow in girth all along their length. As a tree puts on rings it envelops the GL, making the artificial limb even stronger. The tree will eventually push a beam out along the stem of the GL (the reason I prefer a longer stem) in much the same way the tree's roots might lift a heavy concrete sidewalk.

The GL today is a turned-steel device that looks like a billy club with a wide collar starting six inches off a coarsely threaded end. The collar is typically four to six inches wide before it reduces back down and extends another twelve inches or more. It is a heavy piece of hardware that, when screwed into the tree properly, will support enormous weights. There are now many variations on the original GL. They have names like Heavy Limbs and Hyper Limbs, which in various combinations can hold loads as heavy as a 2,700-square-foot house! We are also using mini-GLs and even the poor man's GL, which is a combination of lag bolts, maul washers, and a short sleeve of steel pipe.

In the ten years since the dawn of the GL, Charley Greenwood has been working tirelessly to refine and improve the means of safely attaching heavy structures to trees. His company, Greenwood Engineering, is the only one in the world that specializes in treehouses, so if you need a permit for a particular project, Greenwood is the man to talk to. He will produce a document for you that shows graphically how the house will stay in the tree, and he will back up the claim with page after page of mind-blowing equations. Charley's documents are impressive and we have yet to find a building department that disputes them.

We strongly recommend having any treehouse of significant size engineered by a professional.

Above: Charley Greenwood (center) explaining an engineering feat to Jake Jacob (left) and Daryl McDonald (right).

Above: Occasionally a post is needed to keep a treehouse from overwhelming a tree. This is an engineered "ground strut," as Charley Greenwood, its designer, likes to call it. This one is steel, but they can also be made of wood. Connection to the ground is made with a Diamond Pier, a good way to create strong piers around sensitive root systems. The hole that accommodates the Diamond Pier is only about ten inches deep. Four opposing two-inch galvanized steel pipes driven into the soil with a sledgehammer make the Diamond Piers strong. **Left:** A "heavy limb," also designed by Greenwood, holds up a bucket-style bracket attached to a large glue-laminated beam. There are numerous styles of artificial limbs, or tree anchor bolts (TABs).

CHAPTER 3
Going to School

TREE SELECTION, DESIGN, AND ENGINEERING

The first workshop at Treehouse Point occurred in October of 2006. As the start date was pressing down upon us, it came time to pick a tree and design a house. With so many options it can be difficult to make a decision, but in this case the choice was made for me. Once in a while a blue moon will rise up in the sky and shine upon the tree that is meant to be. That very thing happened one night in late September as I was pondering designs under a fir tree next to the river. While I was imagining the details of that first treehouse on that crisp, clear night (I work best at night), a blue moon came up over the ridge and lit up a neighboring granddaddy Sitka spruce like a light saber in a *Star Wars* movie. It didn't quite dawn on me in the moment, but when I woke up the next morning I knew that the Sitka spruce would host Treehouse Point's first treehouse. It was surely strong enough to support a substantial treehouse, and it was also up and away from the Raging River.

With little time before the workshop began, the pressure was on to design something truly inspired. I dove into my old architecture books and found myself drawn to the vertical lines of the Parthenon in Athens. I'd found the inspiration I was looking for.

As luck would have it, Charley Greenwood happened to be in Seattle the week before our workshop. I held out to him the promise of a years' worth of work if he would please come visit me and do a little seat-of-the-pants engineering on my new plan. He was happy to oblige, and before I knew it I had a platform plan blessed by the man himself. Our first treehouse was off to the races.

MATERIALS

We are blessed in the Northwest with access to ample and outstanding building materials. And with so many wonderful wooden structures being torn down to make way for modern edifices, there are many sustainable choices at our disposal. Half the fun of building a treehouse is coming up with unusual and inexpensive materials to build it.

Right: The plans for the Temple of the Blue Moon were inspired by the Parthenon in Athens. **Opposite:** The Temple of the Blue Moon's name comes from its ancient Greek architectural influence, as well as the fact that its home, the Sitka spruce, was chosen on the night of a blue moon.

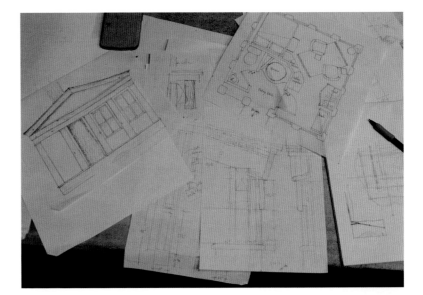

Craigslist is one of the greatest sources for good deals if you look under building materials. You must get in the habit of checking every day, but it is well worth the effort if you know what you are looking for. There are also many outstanding salvage companies filled with used but perfectly good building materials in most cities all over the country. Please support those organizations as well.

CONSTRUCTION

Rigging

In preparation for a platform build, it is wise to spend some time erecting scaffolding, setting rigging, and running safety lines high in the trees. Over the last several years my partner, Jake Jacob, has become proficient at rigging complex block-and-tackle systems that have made life in the field immeasurably easier. They can take time to put in place, but when dealing with heavy loads in areas where a truck or forklift can't gain access, good rigging is the only solution. One can always hire an arborist to set good rigging as well.

Above: During the construction of the Temple of the Blue Moon, overhead rigging allowed us to "float" heavy loads out thirty feet to the evolving platform.
Right: An elegant platform takes shape around the old-growth Sitka spruce. Occasionally a tree will resist a building project, but this magnificent specimen remained calm and allowed us to proceed without protest.

The Platform

The most common issue that arises when working out an effective structure for a tree platform is dealing with large cantilevers. Specifically, treehouses often have two trees in the design, as we do here, and the natural structural solution is to sandwich the trees with two beams and run a joist perpendicular on top. If your trees are a typical twelve to eighteen inches in diameter, in order to fit a decent sized structure on the platform, the main floor joists must cantilever significantly beyond the beams. The solution then is to add a rim joist that runs perpendicular to the main floor joists and then anchor that load back to the tree with four knee braces. That is a perfectly viable solution that can be extremely effective.

However, if the two beams that sandwich the trees could be spread apart more, it's possible to do away with all the knee bracing. This has been my favored objective for a long time mainly because it makes it easier to balance and square up the joist during construction. It also has advantages in terms of tree growth.

It is important to boil down any structural design to its simplest form. Greenwood and I decided on a triangular-shaped spreader, or strut, that would attach to each tree in two places. The beams would rest out on the points of the horizontal part of the triangle. The presumably less elastic side of the Sitka spruce would be statically bolted to the strut, while the other side would rest on plastic skid plates and be captured in its channel by steel tabs. This allows for the beams to move independently of the tree in high wind.

It is also important to note that trees grow awfully quickly. It may not seem like much from year to year, but it adds up fast. I have been stunned by how much wood a tree puts on over time. With all the effort that goes into building a treehouse, the last thing anyone wants to do is spend time five or ten years down the road doing a major structural remodel. A platform plan like this one allows for maximum tree growth. I like to keep main beams at least a foot or more off the bark of any tree. Likewise, I keep joists nine inches off the bark and bring the decking within two inches or so. This way, as the tree grows, you need only break out the jigsaw occasionally and trim away decking rather than move fully loaded joists.

Above: Scaffolding is a very useful tool: Easy to set up, it keeps the job safe and also reduces compaction of the tree's roots. **Below:** A workshop environment can get pretty hectic, but if all the steps are properly choreographed, a lot of work can happen quickly. We even have a cameraman onboard (far right) filming us in anticipation of making a how-to DVD someday.

The Walls and Roof

The column detail on the wall sections needed to be applied before they were hauled into place. Doing as much work as possible on the ground is critical in treehouse construction, as it keeps exposure to a minimum. In this case, there was a fair amount of cutting and grinding that needed to occur to get the organic first-cut cedar slabs to take on a uniform tapered look. Applying them directly to the exterior plywood sheathing took care of a major exterior detail and helped move the project along.

The top plates of the walls are four continuous 4-by-8 beams that run straight to each corner of the building. They double as header beams over the multiple window openings, and they tie the separate wall sections together.

As near as I could measure it, the roof slope of the Parthenon is 3 $\frac{1}{2}$ inches over twelve inches. That is about as low a slope as cedar shake roofing will handle without opening up the possibility of windblown leaks. I like to keep the roof rafters exposed in the interior of a house, so once they were in place, we decked them with 1-by-6 tongue-and-groove fir, added 2-by-8 sections of R-30 ridged insulation, and decked it again with $\frac{5}{8}$ inch CDX plywood. After a layer of heavy-duty waterproofing membrane and some brown metal flashing, it was ready for cedar shakes.

Below: Steve Wray looks on from the spot where the chain bridge will eventually land.

FINISH

Above: Nothing is ever as easy as it looks. Creating the layers of trim on the exterior to mimic Greek design caused plenty of mental and physical anguish. If you want a wood structure to last up in the Northwest, you'd better do a good job of tightening it up against the weather with caulking and flashing. **Left:** Finding correctly sized used widows proved futile, so I bit the bullet and had Lindal, the famous cedar house people, build some new ones. They do a beautiful job and are great to work with. **Center:** Good old cedar board and batten is still my favorite siding material. It goes on quickly, lasts a long time, and looks great with its vertical lines. **Left, below:** The bridge is anchored on the ground side by ten-inch diameter galvanized helical screws that are turned into the earth with a hydraulic drill motor. The screws are typically used to anchor electrical towers, but they are great for starting a chain bridge. Intern Chris Yorke secures sections of decking to the $5/8$ inch chain with $5/8$ inch carriage bolts and lock nuts. **Below:** The interior is finished with 1-by-6 tongue-and-groove fir paneling over rough wiring and insulation. I never use sheetrock on the inside of a treehouse.

Right, above: A queen-size bed is raised
up high in one corner of the room to
create a distinct space. Right, center:
The Northwest Coast Indian moon-face
mask appeared serendipitously in a
trade for some cedar lumber soon after
the treehouse was begun. Right, below:
The wood in our treehouse has stories
to tell. The redwood came from the long
defunct Taylor winery in upstate New
York; the cedar from an old sawmill in
Ketchikan, Alaska; the black walnut in
the floor and armoire came from a tree
cleared for development nearby; and
most of the fir came from second- and
third-growth trees just north of our
town, Fall City, Washington. A door in
another corner leads to a small kidney-
shaped outdoor deck. The bathroom
is opposite the entrance in its own
tiny room. It has only a small sink and
an Incinolet electric toilet. Opposite:
Viewed from below, the Temple of the
Blue Moon appears to be floating in
midair. Overleaf: A path approaches the
spot where the land falls away and an
arboreal world awaits.

Chapter 4

Around the World on a Treehouse Tour

FREE SPIRIT SPHERES

Vancouver Island, British Columbia, Canada

Years ago I was given a book by George Dyson, *Baidarka: The Kayak*, which is a fascinating history of skin boats paddled on the waters of British Columbia and Alaska. Half of the book is dedicated to Dyson's work building modern versions of these classic hunting boats. When he first moved to British Columbia in the 1970s, Dyson had lived for three years in a tiny treehouse at the top of a hundred-foot Douglas fir. In this tree he read books about the Aleuts and the Russian fur trappers or traders, dreaming of their skin-covered boats (called *baidarkas* by the Russians) skimming the cold waters below him. I realized there is a clear parallel between the modern sea kayak and treehouses today: Kayaks are no longer used for hunting just as treehouses are no longer used to keep us safe from predators and flooding, among other things.

Tom Chudleigh of Vancouver Island understands this connection intuitively. Originally conceived as a spherical houseboat, Tom has brought his treehouse design from water to land and into the trees. Called the Free Spirit Sphere, it is an inspired mixture of modern East/West mysticism and the spirit realm of the Inside Passage. The sphere offers an utterly unique experience: "When you're up in the trees, you really get the sense that you are just floating up there, that you're in a different world." Biomimicry, meditative states, and Hundertwasser-like architectural ideals infuse Tom's perspective.

The larger of the two spheres suspended in Tom's trees is ten and a half feet in diameter and made of laminated Sitka spruce covered in fiberglass. Suspended from nylon ropes delicately attached to three trees, it hovers and glows. On first approach, the eye picks out the sphere from quite a distance, but rather than being startled, one smiles from pure delight, having stumbled upon this fantastic vision.

When moving around inside, the sphere sways pleasantly. It also moves slightly when wind bends the treetops, though being suspended from three trees lessens the impact of the breeze. Sleep comes easily, and in the morning one descends to the ground and quickly regains their land legs.

To me, the relation of Tom Chudleigh's ideas to George Dyson's is clear, except that Tom takes us on a journey further down the spiritual path laid out by Dyson: Here in Tom's treehouse we want to travel from one state of mind to another, rather than from one place to another. I'm happy to report, however, that Tom still has plans to float a sphere designed for meditation, massage, and healing on his pond.

Pages 24–25: The path leading to the treehouses at the Nanshan Buddhist Cultural Park on Hainan Island in China.
Above: A large porthole window casts an eye onto a picturesque scene. Acoustics within the spheres are exquisite.
Opposite: A spiral stairway leads to a short suspension bridge. Stepping into the sphere is like stepping onto a boat or into a giant nut.

Right: Boat-style joinery is evident everywhere. The door swings outward on unique hinges that Tom designed and fabricated himself. **Below:** Tom Chudleigh's Free Spirit Spheres are suspended in a grove of trees on the far side of a pond. Tom speaks often of biomimicry, and the concept is evident in the way his spheres blend naturally with their surroundings. **Opposite:** The large sphere, given the name Eryn, hovers above the forest floor. A second, smaller sphere, his prototype, is named Eve since it was the first.

HEIDI'S TREEHOUSE CHALET

Poulsbo, Washington, USA

Instead of opting for a "remuddle," as she calls it, of her storybook cottage on the waters of Puget Sound, Heidi Danilchik convinced her engineer husband, Paul, to consider a treehouse. They needed more space for relaxation and, after adding two bedrooms to their little home, there was simply no room to expand the existing footprint. Paul was excited by the prospect and soon began channeling Heidi's thoughts into drawings.

Their ideas ranged from a hobo-style shack to a full-blown Spanish galleon placed high in two red cedars just up the driveway from the main house. With plans still being sketched, my partner Jake Jacob had a sturdy platform underway. Anna Daeuble at TreeHouse Workshop took over the design, and after a successful collaboration with Heidi, the chalet-style fairy-tale aerie was finally realized on paper. Our trusty carpenter Bubba Smith had an opening in his schedule and everything started falling into place.

At first we were going to build only the stairs and platform, as Paul had planned to finish the rest himself. Heidi's mom was getting on in years and Heidi thought it would be a good idea to create a ramp to allow more universal access. The lay of the land was ideally suited to create such a ramp, and Bubba went to town. With Madrona trees and branches harvested from the property, he wrestled, cut, carved, and created a magical ramp leading up to the platform. But when Heidi saw what Bubba could do, she knew that she wanted him to build the entire treehouse.

From there the project moved forward in phases. Bubba would take working breaks while Heidi and Paul replenished their savings account. All told it took sixteen months to build the 450-square-foot structure.

Heidi loves to share the treehouse and gets the biggest thrill out of watching other people enjoy it. By far the most rewarding aspect of the treehouse for her has been the decision to build a ramp instead of stairs. She claims that the older set goes absolutely wild when they enter the treehouse; many of them never imagined that they would ever set foot in a treehouse again, and for them it is an unexpected dream come true.

Right: One of the most interesting and useful features of Heidi's treehouse is the organic and skillfully crafted ramp that leads to the entry. **Opposite:** The chalet-style treehouse expanded in scope as the platform was being constructed. Additional beams and knee braces were added once the engineer had a chance to catch up to the full design.

Opposite, above: A look into the living room from the bedroom inglenook. Opposite, center: A look from the living room toward the bedroom nook and the lofts above (at left and right). Opposite, below: A queen-size bed rests in the primary loft, while a single bed occupies a separate and smaller loft space directly opposite. Above: A small dining area is tucked in the corner and is open to the kitchen.

Opposite: Planter boxes under windows, among many other details on the tree-house's exterior, nearly overwhelm the senses. **Left:** A cozy front deck overlooks a deep channel in the Puget Sound. **Below:** The foliage of Heidi's beautifully landscaped property nearly obscures the treehouse from view. The low side of the treehouse is nearly twenty feet in the air.

SECRET GARDEN TREEHOUSE

Seattle, Washington, USA

Below: A glass "command center" was added to the tip top of the treehouse when the client and Bubba were reviewing the day's work amidst a half-framed treehouse. **Opposite:** The tree immediately to the left of the cedar stump is actually a sculpted concrete post and chase for electricity. The knothole at the simulated tree's base conceals a light switch.

There is a quiet neighborhood off the beaten path above the locks in Seattle where this hideaway is ensconced. The owner is a young man in the music industry who understands the importance of an inspirational space. Anna Daeuble designed it, and it was built with the skilled hands of Bubba Smith, along with Bubba's brother, Jerrett, and Daryl McDonald.

    The property is an absolutely spectacular setting. The treehouse itself is simply a means for getting up into the air and gaining more enjoyment from the scenery. While I was taking these pictures, a well-fed otter sauntered up and scared me nearly half to death. What beautiful creatures otters are!

Right: Plush leather chairs sit facing a large flat-screen television and some powerful looking stereo speakers. Upstairs, an Aeron office chair is enclosed by glass shelves, walls, and a roof. **Below:** No treehouse would be complete without a place to lie down and catch up on some reading, relaxation, or sleep. There is something soothing and comforting about being surrounded by the rich honey color of tight-grained Douglas fir. **Opposite:** The western red cedars that hold up the treehouse had been badly damaged in a windstorm a few seasons before the treehouse was built. After a visit from a knowledgeable arborist, the trees were saved and given a clean bill of health. They seem to be thriving now.

SQUIRREL'S NEST

Seattle, Washington, USA

I was pulling into the parking lot of Anne's Travel to pick up my tickets to Asia when I came face-to-face with David "Squirrelman" Csaky's make-shift treehouse directly in front of my parking place, high in the branches of a broadleaf maple. It was mid-winter so what would otherwise have been completely obscured by leaves was exposed for all the world to see. I was mesmerized by this structure. The treehouse was clearly the work of an adult, and most likely a homeless one, as there were so many make-shift structures in the empty lots and green spaces in our area, but it was buttoned up tight, and it appeared that no one was there.

A few months passed and just before the leaves started to emerge I returned and had the good fortune of meeting its owner. Unfortunately, it was terrible timing: David had just that morning been served a Notice and Order to Vacate by the City of Seattle. He had built his treehouse on land owned by a power company, and after two years the landowners decided they had had enough. It was time for the treehouse to go. Naturally, Squirrelman was crushed.

How he ended up in a tree is a long and at times sad story. For twenty-eight years David owned a carpet and furniture cleaning business on the East Coast, but after a bitter divorce he decided to move as far away as possible. While on his way to Alaska he got hung-up in Seattle where the Jeep Cherokee he was living in was towed away. Random construction jobs came along, but after being taken advantage of several times, David found himself living on the streets. He was never much of a carpenter, he admits, but he loves animals and nature. After a few attempts at creating a home in the nooks and crannies of the cityscape, he finally settled in an abandoned garage on the waterfront of Lake Union in downtown Seattle. David set to work creating a makeshift living space, which he said looked like a little hunters cabin from the outside, but on the inside was a fully functional apartment. He even had a room for the animals he was fond of taking in and caring for—he had squirrels, a raccoon, two ferrets, and a puppy. One day he returned home from work to find that his home had been bulldozed.

With only two of the ferrets left to keep him company, and a scrap of carpet salvaged from the demolition site, David moved across the street and took refuge in a thicket of briers. For three days he languished in misery with thorns pricking him and various creatures scurrying over and around him at night. He needed to get up and away from his pitiful digs, so he looked to the trees. Though his nerves were shot, he managed to scrounge up a sheet of plywood and a few two-by-fours. He dragged them up a neighboring tree, and a treehouse began to take shape.

That summer the treehouse expanded and went up a story to take advantage of what would've been a million-dollar view. A contractor friend would drop off leftover materials, or David himself would bring stuff home from jobsites. Hammering away under the deafeningly loud Interstate 5 bridge that runs directly overhead, David went undetected until the fall. By that time some of the neighbors had figured out what David was up to and, surprisingly, they approved. Squirrelman is really a gentle soul, and his neighbors began to recognize this and rally around him. One neighbor even went so far as to provide an extension cord for power.

Above: David "Squirrelman" Csaky became an instant celebrity when news of his treehouse hit the front page of the *Seattle Post-Intelligencer.* Here, David looks on, with cameras rolling, while city officials give him a few more days to vacate. **Opposite:** David "Squirrelman" Csaky was able to hammer away all summer on his treehouse, undetected under the deafening noise of the Interstate 5 bridge. The treehouse remained relatively secret until the leaves fell.

By the time I came across him, David was expanding even further: two-by-fours stuck out from the floor with impossible cantilevers, and tarps were stretched and artfully tacked to makeshift rafters. Even in his depressed state that day, his eyes lit up when he showed me around.

The very next day the *Seattle Post-Intelligencer* wrote a story about David and his doomed domicile. His story made the front page. When I returned to take the photos for this book, a line of curious onlookers was waiting for a chance to climb up and say hello. Squirrelman was suddenly a star, and he was beaming. TV cameras were everywhere and the story ended up going out to 134 newspapers around the country. It was a bitter-sweet moment—the treehouse didn't stand a chance, and Squirrelman knew his days in it were numbered, but kindness overflowed, and that afternoon an RV was delivered and donated to David's cause. He no longer needed to worry about where he would live.

David is now living in his RV north of Seattle and is helping at an animal shelter. He has more animals than ever to take care of now, and he tells me the views go on forever. It's terrific to hear that he's finally landed on his feet.

Opposite: There is something graceful about David's creation. Treehouse living isn't for everyone, but it suited him just fine. **Left, above:** While David's treehouse had no walls to speak of, he nevertheless had everything he needed to survive the mild Seattle winters. His home lasted two of them before the cold hand of the law swept his arboreal abode away. **Left, below:** Within the open walls of David's hideout there is an inner sanctum that is more weather tight. It is basically a camping tent where he sleeps and keeps his pet ferret, rat, and squirrel.

PAT AND LORI'S TREEHOUSE

Western Washington, USA

Many people we have built for are self-made something-or-others, and we have worked like mad to make their dreams come true. Pat owns a specialized data company and has done very well for himself. Building for clients like this is always fun, and Pat and Lori were no exception.

Pat is into bridges and trains, so one day he brought Carroll Vogel, owner of Sahale Bridge Builders in Seattle, to his property with the hope of building a full-blown bridge. Unfortunately, his property slopes away in all directions, so at first they thought there was nothing to bridge to. Then Carroll suggested sending a bridge to a pair of massive fir trees at the property's edge. Pat was intrigued, and soon TreeHouse Workshop was called upon to come up with a design for a treehouse. The two projects were to go on concurrently—the bridge was started first to provide a main connection.

It was a while before the project for the bridge got underway, and in the meantime the treehouse plan was developed and refined. The main part of the treehouse would rest on the last of four bridge abutments. As Sahale Bridge Builders installed the final abutment, treehouse building began in earnest.

Every now and then Pat would show up after work, always in a pair of shorts. "I only wear pants for skiing and funerals," he says. He would get a gleam in his eye as we discussed details regarding the next stage of construction. His interest and excitement about the process was always a pleasure to watch.

Below: A full-scale steel bridge was the impetus for building the treehouse.
Opposite: Pat had no place to land his dream bridge until it was suggested by the bridge builder that he could land it in the two beautiful Douglas fir trees on the edge of his property where the treehouse now sits.

Above: The deck on the back of the treehouse is thirty-five feet above the ground. **Right:** A bridge abutment lands a safe distance from the roots of two mature Douglas fir trees. The bridge carries half the weight of the treehouse while the two trees carry the other half with strong, highly flexible connections. **Opposite:** This grand treehouse is used primarily as a kids' hangout, though the adults are known to spend time there, too. It took five months to build and is estimated to weigh 80,000 pounds.

SHARA'S TREEHOUSE

Issaquah, Washington, USA

A few years before we built their treehouse, Shara and Scott participated in one of our first workshops in Fall City. Scott didn't get the attendance award that year (he is a very busy local executive), but his wife, Shara, is a diligent worker and a wisecracker who knows what she likes and possesses beguiling ways of getting it. When the call came in that it was time to start planning Shara's treehouse, we jumped at the chance.

Shara is an excellent visual planner. We spent a lot of time pacing off spaces in her living room to help her visualize the actual size of the plan we were conjuring up for her. First it was too small, then it was too expensive. Scott has an accountant's background, so he is the practical counterpart. One thing I will say about the process of designing a treehouse is that the the more I can share and collaborate with a client the more enjoyable it is. Treehouses tend to be spontaneous creations, but a good plan at the start is one of the best ways to ensure that a treehouse the client loves will be the final outcome.

The above notwithstanding, the project evolved beyond the plan. For one thing, though the hot tub was always going to be integral to the house, it was not clear exactly where it was supposed to end up. The zip line, a cable stretched between trees that "zips" down by way of a specialized trolley that is attached to the waist by a climbing harness, was a logical addition that necessitated a small bridge and two more small platforms. It also turned out that the treehouse itself, originally intended to be a card room or a changing room for hot-tubbing, somehow evolved into Scott's home office. Shara still commandeers it for the occasional nap, and in any capacity it's a pretty cool space.

Below: This is Shara's view of the treehouse from her kitchen window.
Opposite: The house floats on four Douglas fir trees and one broadleaf maple. Wind was a consideration in this location so maximum flexibility was built into the substructure.

Below: Stairs descend from the main platform to the hot tub deck and then a bridge connects to the zip line platform. A strong nylon net is stretched below the start of the zip line for an added measure of safety.

Opposite, above: In addition to the office, there is a loft bed along with a couch and television for rest and relaxation. The walls and ceiling are all crafted from Douglas fir.

Opposite, below: Scott set up a plush office in the treehouse soon after the project was completed. Originally the treehouse was going to be a card room, changing room, and refuge, but a job offer came along that the family could not resist, so Scott now does some telecommuting via treehouse.

THE DRIFTWOOD INN

South Puget Sound, Washington, USA

Tucked into a ravine that opens into a remote channel of the Puget Sound, this treehouse gestated for ten years before it was finally built. Bryan, the owner, has a stunning weekend house on the same property but found it lacked that all-important playful element. With his two young sons in mind, he turned his attention to a pair of mature Douglas firs that reside behind his workshop. Having built makeshift treehouses from old doors as a boy, it was time to start planning the real thing.

A huge part of the fun of building a treehouse is planning it. Bryan helped out in that department, and drew plans for fifty different designs, but he suffered from too much of a good thing—a wealth of ideas—and couldn't decide on one. He called on me to put an end to that phase of the job and to start putting some wood in the trees.

Both parties came away pleased with the results. Bryan's boys named the treehouse the Driftwood Inn, and it is used regularly for game playing and sleepovers. Dad stays downstairs on the hide-a-way and the boys stay upstairs in the bunk room, often with a few friends.

Right: A comfortable deck wraps around the side and back of the treehouse. The deck on the side is covered, while the large deck in the back is open to the elements. A huge Douglas fir comes up through this deck. My guess is that a tree this size is only about one hundred years old; they grow quickly in the Northwest. **Opposite:** The Driftwood Inn juts proudly into a wild ravine.

Right, above: The bridge was created with chain, cedar planks, Hemp-x rope, and custom steel brackets that double as railing posts. Right, below: The carriage was engineered not only for plumbing and electrical but also to carry an enormous load, estimated for engineering purposes at 135,000 pounds. Opposite: The setting sun draws a beautiful hue from the cedar board-and-batten siding.

Right: Complementing the exposed beams, driftwood logs and tree bark are featured throughout the treehouse. **Below:** Fully plumbed, the Driftwood Inn features a functional kitchen and bathroom. **Opposite, above:** The second floor is full of clever ways to maximize space, such as lots of built-in drawers and secret compartments. It is both a perfect play and sleep area for kids and a useful guest room for adults. **Opposite, below:** The main floor sitting area is right next to the open kitchen and is a great place to enjoy a glass of wine or a cold beer while the kids play. **Overleaf:** The Driftwood Inn and its three magnificent Douglas firs. Notice the space allowed for growth around each of the trees where the structure embraces them.

TRILLIUM TREEHOUSE

Fall City, Washington, USA

Back at Treehouse Point a second treehouse is taking shape. This one is a daring design that hangs off to one side of a massive western red cedar. Trillium Treehouse was started during a five-day workshop at the Northwest Treehouse School and is slowly nearing completion as time and money allows.

Right: A second-story loft that covers one half of the eight-by-sixteen-foot floor plan will house an elaborate queen-size bed and electric toilet. Downstairs there's room for two reading chairs, a closet, bookshelves, a writing desk, and a small kitchen. Not bad for two hundred square feet. **Opposite:** The spiral staircase that winds around the cedar is a gradual trip over and above a trout pond, which sits at the base of the tree, and up to the front door of this more contemporary structure.

RODERICK ROMERO

The first time Roderick came to see us in Fall City, he was armed with a portfolio that included a treehouse in Italy for the rock star Sting. My kids were fascinated by Roderick's incredibly long black ponytail, blazing smile, and the intricate color tattoos covering his arms.

Since that fateful evening, TreeHouse Workshop has been the lucky benefactor of Roderick's prodigious design skills. Mr. Romero consistently finds interesting and often famous clients, and after he designs and prices his creations, he calls in the TreeHouse Workshop team to implement them. We have had some wonderful experiences together in far-flung places.

One thing about Mr. Romero—he makes stuff happen. He is a bit like a symphony conductor who leads the group yet at the same time allows everyone to play as their hearts direct them. He trusts in the experience and permits his art to evolve on its own as the project develops. When he latches onto an idea or a theme or simply something that resonates with him, he is sure to see it through. In the process friendships are forged and great art is made.

I've selected a few of his amazing treehouses for this book—Lantern House, Petra Cliff Treehouse, the Darna School Treehouse (page 158), and Finca Bellavista (page 138). Enjoy!

LANTERN HOUSE
Santa Monica, California, USA

In the case of Christiana's project in the Santa Monica Mountains, Roderick's muse was a Moroccan lantern. His otherworldly creation really does mimic one of those beautiful glowing tin lanterns.

As in all of Roderick's buildings, salvaged and reclaimed materials are an integral part of the structure. This was important to the client, who is involved in her own eco-friendly businesses. The redwood came from old olive oil barrels, and the windows came from a salvage yard in North Hollywood. Even the stairway was salvaged—it came from a tree that was threatening to fall on a nearby road. Roderick had noticed a road crew removing the tree and asked if he could have a long section of the trunk. It was quite an effort to get it into place, but it makes one heck of a staircase. Daryl McDonald and Dayle West, the two lead carpenters on the job, along with one of Roderick's closest friends of old, Jeff Casper, remember vividly the day they put it in place.

Roderick's signature "live" railing was added in the final phase of construction. Eucalyptus limbs were harvested from throughout the property and woven together to create an intricate and complex railing that is infused with joy. I got to visit this wonderful place over Earth Day weekend in 2007, and I must say that climbing up the cocoonlike stairway was a singular experience. That great book of the unspoken laws of architecture, *A Pattern Language* by Christopher Alexander, talks of creating decompression zones before entering a home, be it a turn in an approach path or a landing on a stair. This tunnel of beautifully woven branches serves that function—it signals that you are leaving one world and entering into a new one.

Left: A fantastic woven web of eucalyptus branches leads up and away from earthbound encumbrances.
Below: Three mature eucalyptus trees balance Lantern House between their massive trunks.

PETRA CLIFF TREEHOUSE

Pecos, New Mexico, USA

One day the actress Julianne Moore called Roderick to let him know that the actor Val Kilmer might soon be calling him about a treehouse. Sure enough, about an hour later, Mr. Kilmer called and invited Roderick to his enormous ranch in New Mexico. The flight from New York didn't take long, but it took Roderick four days of overland trekking across six thousand acres before he finally settled on a four-oak outcropping just above the lovely Pecos River. Mr. Kilmer arrived on the fifth day, gave Roderick his blessing, and the show was on.

When the A-team arrived—Daryl McDonald and Bubba Smith, plus their friend Carlos Beuth—there was enough material that Roderick had amassed to complete the platform. The materials for the house itself, however, were still to be determined. An ancient barn had caught Roderick's eye ten miles down the road, so while the A-team went to work swinging hammers, Roderick went to work securing salvage rights to the derelict barn. It took him five days, but once he convinced the old rancher that the material was to be respectfully reused, he had enough material to build three treehouses.

In the meantime, juniper trees were harvested to create an artistic roof-rafter system. Rusty metal from the old barn was reused on the treehouse roof and even hammered out and installed on the face of the entry door. There is no glass in this simple one-room treehouse; shutters with cactus trim protect the interior from the often howling winds.

Below: Oak branches twist and wind through the railing of a perfect hideout on the Pecos River. **Opposite:** Nestled at the base of a sandstone cliff, Val Kilmer's rustic treehouse has the look of a reclusive miner's cabin.

Opposite, above: These doors, fabricated from a locally salvaged barn, appear to have been built in the 1880s. Opposite, below: With doors flung open, a single rudimentary room is revealed. Left: Shutters drop down to expose the fabulous views out across the scrubland. Below: Whimsical materials, like the dried cactus husks that trim the shutters and the sun-worn metal roofing, come together to create an eccentric and arresting amalgamation of materials.

EUCALYPTUS TREEHOUSE
Los Angeles, California, USA

There is a lot to be said for the mossy wet climes of the great Northwest, but come April, when it's still forty-two degrees outside and the rain is coming down sideways, the prospect of building in Los Angeles becomes terribly seductive. I have heard myself in mid-winter conversations with those happy, warm people in California, literally begging them to let me come down for a look at their property.

One such unsuspecting client called on a particularly chilly April morning. My cover was blown, I am sure, when I eagerly offered to arrive at their home the next morning. Nonetheless, they graciously received me and before the week was out we had the go ahead for an inspired structure that would be used as a young girls' hideaway.

Right: This cozy treehouse reveals nothing of the light-filled interior. Because the family's main house sits on the top of a bluff, the girls must walk down a gradual pathway to their own little house tucked in the eucalyptus trees.
Opposite: The windows and curved walls give this treehouse the feel of a mountaintop lookout. The view goes on for miles.

Opposite: Salvaged fir floors and studs frame red cedar siding boards. **Left:** Blake Warner crafted walnut stools to match a walnut slab writing desk and a shark-fin-shaped counter-top. **Below:** The rafters converge on a ridge beam like ribs on a keel of a wooden boat.

Above: The shape of this treehouse was inspired by the curved walls of the main house. **Opposite:** The main house sits at the top of a bluff, the treehouse sits below it, and the rest of the property slopes down even further, creating a dramatic setting for the treehouse.

KIT AND KAREN'S TREEHOUSE

San Diego County, California, USA

Owners Kit and Karen had us build this fully appointed treehouse—our largest to date—after a friend dared Kit to do it. We're glad he took the dare! After a few years of research, and many tours of TreeHouse Workshop projects, they got their dream off the ground east of San Diego, California.

Engineered by Charley Greenwood and built in seven trees (two of which were fabricated), this one-thousand-square-foot treehouse was TreeHouse Workshop's first to employ steel beams. Carpenter Bubba Smith demonstrated his mastery while living out his Tarzan fantasy in a small treehouse, which he built for himself on-site while the project was going on and tore down when it was finished. He spent nine months creating Kit and Karen's bungalow-in-the-trees, and even fell in love with TreeHouse Workshop's own Anna Daeuble, who is now his wife.

Kit and Karen's treehouse narrowly escaped a blaze as it was being completed in 2004, but sadly, in 2007, it took only a few short minutes to burn down to nothing. "You could fit the ashes into a quart bottle," says Kit. Thankfully, no one from the group was hurt on that fateful day when the wildfires were devouring half of San Diego County.

Below: This organic structure seems to have settled into the arms of these old California oaks. The combination of beautiful woodworking by one of our master carpenters, and the heavy masonry fireplace, which anchors the treehouse into the ground, is a nod to the Arts and Crafts period. **Opposite, above:** A nicely placed chair from which to contemplate Bubba's extraordinary railing. **Opposite, below:** The third tree from the right is actually fabricated from wood lath, chicken wire, and concrete. On the left is the base of the large fireplace. **Overleaf:** The supporting trees naturally curve out from the platform and complement the rustic railing. Live-edged siding enhances the horizontal lines of the structure. All the siding was harvested from dead oaks on-site and cut with a Wood-Mizer portable sawmill.

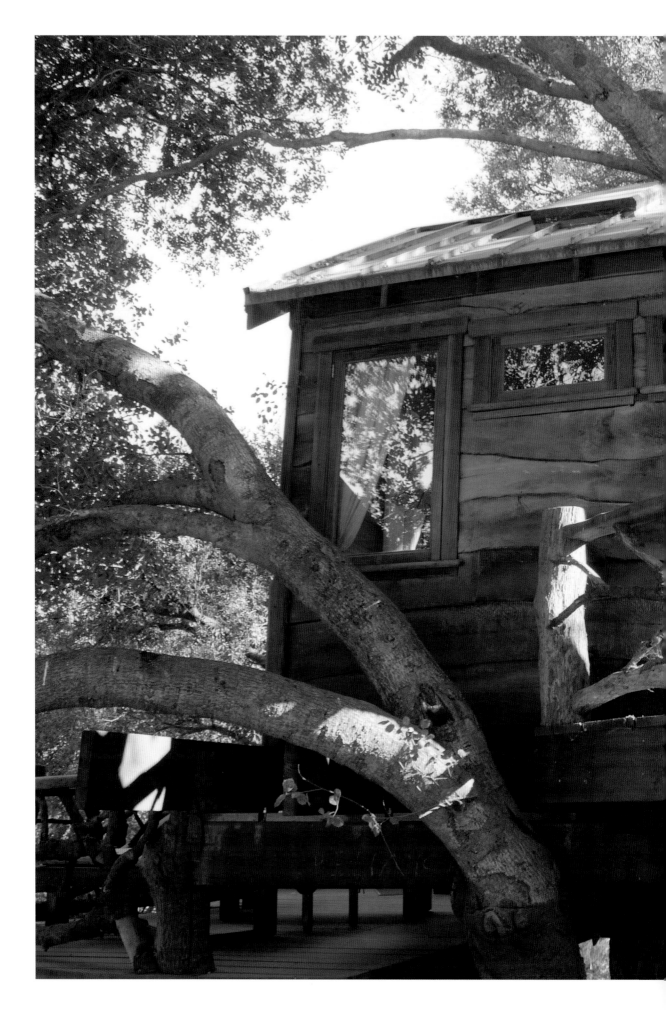

HORACE'S CATHEDRAL

Crossville, Tennessee, USA

Horace Burgess received his mission from God in approximately four seconds one fateful night eighteen years ago. In that short moment of clairvoyance, a vision of an enormous treehouse-church presented itself to him, with almost every imaginable detail intact. After receiving this vision, Horace knew that his life had changed forever, and that it would be for God's glory that the most amazing treehouse ever built would come from his own two hands.

Now fifty-eight years of age, Horace wonders where the energy to build the cathedral came from. It took fifteen years to build and he is still working on it. As I stood with him one beautiful spring day, I watched as his "Burgess blue eyes" roamed the intricate expanse of its façade; we looked upon a church that quite simply blows the mind.

Right: Old acetylene bottles are hung from wire and used as bells in a belfry that reaches up ninety-seven feet.
Opposite: Wood from five different barns went into the creation of Horace's Cathedral. It has taken him fifteen years to build so far, and at fifty-eight he is showing little sign of slowing down.

Opposite: Like several others in the edifice, a remnant oak tree was long ago enveloped by the church and is now void of life but still supports the structure. The church pulpit is at left and sits at the foot of the crucifix. The choir sits in the wooden bleachers on the right. **Left:** A spiral stair tunnels up and around a grand white oak. Bits of scrap wood pepper the walls both inside and out creating a unique and beautiful wicker-like texture. **Below:** When church is not in service, the space doubles as a basketball court. A few pews are to the right of the red, white, and blue basket, which is directly opposite the crucifix.

Above: An enormous corrugated plastic skylight illuminates the nave of Horace's Cathedral. **Opposite:** The treehouse generally follows the lines of an enormous white oak until the tree's branches burst out of the structure like unruly hair. In the summer the treehouse is mostly obscured by foliage.

RACHEL'S TREEHOUSE
Abingdon, Virginia, USA

I first encountered Rachel Fowlkes at the 2002 World Treehouse Association Conference in Oregon. She came with her tall, affable boyfriend, Don, all the way from Abingdon, Virginia, with plenty of questions and a strong desire to understand the concept of building in a tree. An innovator and a real go-getter, Rachel was the founder of a fully fledged university in rural Virginia, the Southwest Virginia Higher Education Center. I was honored to get her call a few months after the conference inviting me to come and see where she wanted to build her treehouse.

Rachel's land—more than a hundred acres—has it all. Forested hills roll down to open fields and then through more forest down to the south fork of the Holston River. The famous Virginia Creeper Trail winds its way along the bank, and mature trees provide an ideal location for a treehouse. The beech trees in that part of the forest are truly astounding—they have always been one of my favorite trees. Unfortunately, the one I had my eyes on had a double trunk and an arborist felt that it posed a risk of splitting. We ultimately decided to build in a stout pin oak, which was chosen for its location more than anything else.

Two years later, we were ready to build. The basic spatial layout of a treehouse can arise quickly once the tree or trees have been identified. It's the platform that tends to take more time and effort. In this case, treehouse engineering guru Charley Greenwood was called to town. We needed a building permit, and Charley is the only one I know in the entire country who will provide the all-important engineer's stamp of approval for a tree-based structure. We were lucky to have him, but at one point we felt like wringing his neck for making the connection to the tree nearly impossible to install.

But thankfully, construction of this treehouse was placed in the very capable hands of one of our most patient carpenters, Bubba Smith, who'd taken a shine to Rachel (as most of us did) when we'd first visited the site

Above: The back porch overlooks the Holston River and the famous Virginia Creeper Trail. **Right:** The entrance welcomes visitors who must first traverse a long bridge made safe by Bubba's fantastical rustic railings. **Opposite:** Rachel's two-story tower tapers six inches over its seventeen-foot wall height. It was time consuming to cut all the wall studs with a taper, but so much easier on the eyes.

two years before. Don is still in the picture, mind you, but the treehouse was a match made in heaven. We threw in the talents of a few others, namely Anna Daeuble, Ben Smith (no relation to Bubba), and a lighting specialist by the name of Woody Crenshaw. In the end, it was Bubba who made this treehouse sing.

A bridge leads to this peaceful getaway. Inside the treehouse it is absolutely tranquil. Natural light flows into the room, illuminating the warmth of the fir woodwork. Luxurious and completely habitable, the treehouse is equipped with a fully functioning bathroom and kitchen replete with hot and cold running water.

Rachel now has plans to build a few more treehouses, including a café that would feed some of the 200,000 annual trekkers on the Creeper Trail.

Opposite: A Western red cedar countertop glows in the small kitchen. The rest of the wood is all clear vertical grain Douglas fir with a clear finish. **Left:** A tiny gas fireplace puts out enough heat to keep the 420 square foot treehouse completely comfortable. **Overleaf, left:** Bubba harvested some wild cherry on the property and used it for the posts holding up the stairway. They are a natural counterbalance to the otherwise sharp lines of the overall design. **Overleaf, right:** The living room is surrounded on three sides by walls of windows and brings the outdoors inside.

FOREVER YOUNG TREEHOUSES

Vermont, USA

I think of Bill Allen, founder of Forever Young Treehouses, as a Johnny Appleseed for this generation of handicapped and physically challenged individuals. Maybe it's the fact that he is from Burlington, Vermont, which reminds me of winesap apples and cider, but Bill and his team, consisting of designer James "B'fer" Roth and builder Eyrick Stauffer, are sprinkling the country with stunning, universally accessible treehouses.

A former insurance agent and former director of the Make-a-Wish Foundation of Vermont, Bill has mastered the art of raising money, navigating bureaucratic red tape, and removing engineering obstacles. He is also adept at orchestrating massive volunteer work crews. His easygoing spirit inspires everyone he encounters, and his determination has resulted in the building of many wonderful projects. Forever Young won't meet their stated goal of "a treehouse in every state by 2008," but undaunted, they are trying to come up with a battle cry that rhymes with "2010."

"When you stop to think about it," Bill has been known to say, "a treehouse is one of the most exclusive clubs in the world. Forever Young is trying to change all that."

SCRANTON TREEHOUSE

Scranton, Pennsylvania, USA

Forever Young has treehouses in nineteen states at this point, but they have more than one in some states. In this instance, the universally accessible ramp actually slopes *down* to a treehouse that is thirty feet off the ground. It feels much higher than that because the treehouse is on the edge of a basalt gorge that plunges another two hundred feet to a river below.

Above: Designed by B'fer Roth, this treehouse seems to hover in the trees. **Right:** In order to comply with the American Disabilities Act ramp slope requirements (one foot rise or fall for every twelve feet of horizontal distance), long bridges stretch to Forever Young treehouses. To break up the journey, allow traffic to eddy, and give space to enjoy different vistas, this bridge widens as it passes each tree. **Opposite:** I love how whimsical and light this treehouse is. It is so light, in fact, that it was retrofitted with cables to reduce swaying. **Overleaf, left:** The floor and ramp of the treehouse are made of Ipe wood, which is extremely durable. It also has an interesting property in that its grain rises in wet weather to create a non-skid surface. The natural posts are stripped eastern white cedar and the rood framing is made entirely of Douglas fir. **Overleaf, right:** Steel posts with "branches" carry one side of the treehouse, raising it high above a stunning gorge.

LONGWOOD GARDENS

Kennett Square, Pennsylvania, USA

Longwood Gardens in Kennett Square, Pennsylvania, is a horticultural center and a public garden with a rich history. Pierre DuPont saved the forest that was originally on this land from loggers in 1909 and turned it into his summer home. He then expanded his land holdings from two hundred acres to more than a thousand acres and built magnificent gardens as well as a glorious conservatory. Fortunately for all of us, DuPont formed a private foundation to manage the property after his death in the 1950s, and today the gardens are open to the public. The gardens receive more than 800,000 visitors every year, but the new director, Paul Redmond, felt a need to reach out to young visitors beyond the local garden clubs. When Sharon Loving, the director of horticulture at the gardens, handed Paul a copy of my first book along with the idea of building a treehouse, he jumped on it.

CANOPY CATHEDRAL

In February of 2007, I was at Longwood Gardens during what turned out to be the biggest snowstorm of the season. Walking through their awe-inspiring conservatory with snow piled up outside was truly a magical experience! Having been directed to design two treehouses in two separate areas of the gardens, I was immediately taken by the statuesque beauty of the massive tulip poplar trees, which are said to date back to the days of George Washington. Some of these were four feet around with not a branch below fifty feet. The design for the treehouse I would build popped into my head instantly. I had once visited an exact reproduction of a Norwegian stave church in Moorhead, Minnesota; it was one of the most beautiful and fascinating wooden structures I had ever seen. Now, walking among the tulip poplars at Longwood Gardens, it seemed to me that the ancient design would perfectly complement this regal stand of trees. In a matter of minutes I had a sketch drawn up of Canopy Cathedral. It took a lot longer to build!

Above: A friendly dragon, the work of Oregon carver Caleb McGregor, guards the entrance. **Right:** A treehouse of this size and function was designed with more than just beauty in mind; traffic flow was also a consideration. Three doors invite visitors in from the large deck. **Opposite:** The Canopy Cathedral required some serious engineering: The foundation consists of thirty-four steel posts with Diamond Piers. Even more difficult was turning the enormous picture window in my original drawing into a reality. **Overleaf, left:** The symmetrical design complements the post-and-beam construction used in medieval stave churches. **Overleaf, right:** Carved cedar railings and wide-plank cedar treads lead past maple, cherry, and grand tulip poplar trees to this church-like house in the trees.

THE BIRD HOUSE

The second treehouse we built at Longwood Gardens was to be completely different from the first, and we decided to make it a little more playful. Again we had a beautiful stand of ancient tulip poplars to play in, but this time we were deep in a forest. Now we had the chance to go *up*.

Since no penetrations into the trees were allowed, it was decided that a light steel frame would carry the house. A stairway would wind around the tree up to where you could get an absolutely new perspective of the forest. Standing on the deck of the treehouse was to feel like you were at a cocktail party with some giant friends.

Right: The art of the steel frame shines here, built by Engineering, Inc., of Wilmington, Delaware. **Opposite:** Inspired by fire lookout towers, the Bird House gets visitors up high so they have a panoramic view of the forest.

Above: A soft path and hand-hewn gate invite visitors to climb the stairs.
Right: The tulip poplar that defines this treehouse continues skyward through a hole in the roof.

Left: A sliding barn door made from western red cedar with a rhodedendrum branch for a handle opens up the interior, making this modest treehouse feel larger than it is. **Below:** Looking into the woods from twenty feet up gives one a new perspective that is usually reserved only for the birds.

LOOKOUT LOFT

I first heard from Bill Allen, founder of Forever Young Treehouses, about ten years ago when he called to tell me about his vision to build treehouses for children and young adults with special needs. We became fast friends, but this Longwood Gardens project in 2007 was our first collaboration. In truth, our treehouses at Longwood were separate endeavors, but when Forever Young wrapped theirs up early, their builder, Eyrick Stauffer, was happy to lend TreeHouse Workshop a much needed hand so that we could finish ours on schedule.

Forever Young's Lookout Loft complies with the Americans with Disabilities Act, which requires one inch of rise for every foot of ramp. In this case, the natural slope of the forest walk worked very much in their favor.

Opposite: Milled lumber, shaped steel, stripped logs, and glue-laminated beams, not to mention the tulip poplars themselves, are just some of the materials used to create the Lookout Loft. **Left, above:** From beneath its canopy one can see across a large, undulating meadow. **Left:** The roof arcs delicately and lightly, as though it were a leaf or wing caught in an updraft. **Below:** Using vines harvested from the surrounding forest is a creative way to decorate and protect the growth space left around the tulip poplar.

TEPEE TREEHOUSE

Eastern Pennsylvania, USA

My partner Jake Jacob never ceases to amaze me with the depth of his connections around this country. When we were in Kennett Square, Pennsylvania, checking out the site in Longwood Gardens, we toyed with the idea of bringing in a local timber framer to help out. It just so happened that Jake knew a timber-framing pioneer who lived right outside of town. We rolled into Hugh Lofting's shop that sunny spring afternoon, and as soon as he heard what we were up to a big smile spread across his face: "I just finished a treehouse right up the road. Wanna go see it?" Next thing I knew, we were on some property that will go down in my memory as one of the most beautiful I have ever visited.

The property's owner had hatched the idea of building a treehouse with her brother-in-law, Attie Jonker, who runs a design company that dabbles in whimsical building projects. Together they conspired to build a treehouse for children with a Native American theme. Attie, who grew up in South Africa and spent nearly ten years designing remote safari camps in places like Botswana, guided Hugh's crew.

A sturdy white oak holds the treehouse up, and almost everything in the structure is salvaged or reclaimed. The green oak beams were harvested locally; the flooring and roof rafters were salvaged from a nearby barn. It has a wide-open floor plan with enough room in a loftlike space above to sleep a small army of children. Everywhere there are wonderful details, from the sharply pointed rafter tails to the sharp pegs that adorn the sidewall panels next to the main entry door. A great deal of care and effort went into making this a very special building.

Below: Sharpened rafter tails and intricate railing details merely hint at the complexity of a project like this. Treehouses always take several months to build, and this one was no exception. **Opposite:** The Native American theme employed by designer Attie Jonker comes through in the tepee-like roof of the treehouse. **Overleaf, left:** I had assumed that the side panels next to the front door were surely artifacts from an old farm, but the designer explained that they had created the sharp, pointed adornments purely for visual impact. **Overleaf, right:** A fabricated tree holds up tightly spaced rafters that were salvaged from a local one hundred-year-old barn. **Pages 110–111:** A stunningly picturesque Pennsylvania farm spreads out below the deck of this children's treehouse.

THE MARSH HOUSE

Long Island, New York, USA

Okay, so the Marsh House is not in a tree. It sits on stilts, though you can't see them. It is also among the top five most influential buildings in my life. I started noticing this little hideaway when I was all of ten years old, wandering the salt marshes looking for painted turtles. It went through a major overhaul and remodeling many years ago, and the owner, Michael Ince, was nervous about presenting it for fear of having the buildings department come down on him, but enough time has passed, and we agreed that it was time for more people to delight in its beauty.

Michael Ince is an artist and sculptor who lives on the Great South Bay of Long Island. He builds the most beautiful wooden sculptures, including the occasional treehouse (which have been featured in my previous books), but to me this "treehouse" is his masterwork. The Marsh House is a satellite to his main home, but it sparkles with all the magic and intimacy of his larger spaces.

Many times I have attempted to capture the spirit of Michael's buildings in my own work, but never have I come close. In architecture so many things that make the heart sing are indescribable and the way Michael transforms a functional retreat into a place brimming with natural beauty and harmony is one of them. To me his buildings are too beautiful for words.

Below: The entry to Michael's Marsh House playfully warns intruders to keep out while at the same time seducing them to come closer to have a look. The details in this house are fantastic. **Opposite, above:** A back porch overlooks a preserved salt marsh on the Great South Bay of Long Island. In my youth I spent countless hours combing this mysterious wonderland for turtles and buried treasure. **Opposite, below:** What was once a simple structure was magically transformed by owner Michael Ince into the treasure I had always been seeking.

FALCON'S PERCH

Long Island, New York, USA

When we sent Bubba Smith to the tip of Long Island's south shore with Anna Daeuble to assemble a children's playhouse, I think only she was aware of the potential at the time. I see this exquisite little treehouse as a duet in which each of them sang their piece. Anna's playful hand drafted the lines of the building while Bubba's deft carpentry skills faithfully softened every edge. It was a dance, in a way, and now a piece of their two hearts stands in the front yard of a beautiful home in Long Island. When I see the harmony in this treehouse, I realize I should've known then that Bubba and Anna would eventually get married.

Opposite, above: Master carver Douglas McGregor of Oregon crafted the two falcons that give this treehouse its name.
Opposite, below: Rarely does a collaboration result in such a harmonious creation. Bubba's wood working skills made all of the subtle curves in Anna's design come to life.
Below: A large cherry tree carries this treehouse elegantly with the help of two GLs, a few cables, and four sculpted posts.

Right, above: The front stairway leads directly into a glowing playroom where tight-grained Douglas fir was used exclusively. **Right:** The playroom feels as much like a chapel as it does a place to read books and stack blocks. **Opposite:** A pocket door (ingeniously pocketless) leads inside from the front deck. A ship's ladder takes one to the shoebox sleeping loft.

THE TREEHOUSE

Pound Ridge, New York, USA

Something about this treehouse brings a smile to everyone's face when they first see it. Is it the setting or the structure that people find so appealing? Years ago I was given a powerful book about treehouses written in the mid-'70s by the staff of Green Tiger Press entitled *Treehouses: An Illustrated Essay on the Aesthetic & Practical Aspects of Arboreal Architecture.* They write: "To be in a treehouse is to be inside and yet outside, to be free and yet protected, to be up in the air and yet rooted, held. It is a distant retreat yet conveniently near. It is being adventurous and yet home-loving, a wayfarer and nest builder, a pirate and lighthouse keeper. Treehouses enclose all the spirit that needs enclosure and liberates all the spirit that needs to see horizon to horizon and guess what lies beyond." I think that captures why this treehouse speaks to us all.

Above: Playful curves in the entry door and barge boards soften the appearance of this treehouse and delight the eye. **Right:** A trapdoor that can be opened from below with a rope is the only way to the deck of the treehouse. An old scythe mounted on the wall above the trapdoor opening provides a sturdy hand hold to assist in the final ascent to the platform. **Opposite:** Anna Daeuble of TreeHouse Workshop designed this gem of a treehouse. It was built in kid scale so everything about it is small and tight.

Opposite: One hundred percent of the materials used in building this treehouse were salvaged or recycled. **Left:** The downstairs has everything a child might need to make any day a beautiful one. **Below:** The upstairs is reached by a tiny spiral staircase. There is enough room for a few children to sleep, but that is about it.

SOLACE TREEHOUSE
Western New Jersey, USA

Dan Mack is an artist who has been working with wood for thirty years. He is also a rustic furniture maker and an author. I have admired his work for many years, so when I heard he was building a treehouse, I became excited.

Dan has been working for this client for years, creating all kinds of whimsical structures both large and small on this weekend property in western New Jersey. The inspiration for a treehouse came from a solitary behemoth of a sycamore tree that stands majestically in the lower side yard. If any tree begs for a treehouse, it's this one. It's branches spread from its massive trunk at just the right height to be both dangerously high and surprisingly comfortable in its branchy perch. Dan heard the call and soon the client was on board. They even brought TreeHouse Workshop into the fold to help engineer and build the platform. The result is pure delight.

The treehouse was built way up in the air in the "hobo style," as Dan calls it, and on a scale that accommodates this six-foot-four patron. There are wonderful old newspapers papering the walls throughout the interior, and it has the comfortable feel of an old boxcar turned secret hideout.

Above: A cable that is attached to a window washer's bosun chair hanging outside threads through second-story floorboards on its way to the spool of an electric winch that is bolted to the floor below. **Right:** The finely crafted bosun's chair hangs from a gimbaled arm that can be maneuvered to wash windows on the exposed sides of the house. **Opposite:** Artist and woodworker Dan Mack designed and built this sprawling treehouse in the branches of a massive sycamore tree. His brilliant natural creations fill this entire weekend property, but the tree-house is his crowning achievement.

Opposite: A view into the living room from above; everything appears to have been in place for ages. **Above:** Very old newspapers adorn the walls and serve as instant reminders of bygone eras. **Left:** Rustic furnishings adorn the interior of the house, including this beautiful lamp. The lampshade seems to have been attracting the attention of squirrels. **Overleaf, left:** Rustic details abound in this full-scale arboreal home. The client is a tall man and Dan Mack needed to be sure it would accommodate him comfortably. Unfortunately, the treehouse is also accommodating some unwelcome squirrels and a battle to evict them is raging on. **Overleaf, right:** I climbed a neighboring tree to get a shot of the back of the treehouse. This is the kind of place I dreamed about as a kid.

ANDREW THURNHEER'S TREEHOUSE
Danby, New York, USA

After Andrew Thurnheer had finished guiding me by cell phone up his commanding hillside in upstate New York, I stepped out of my rental car to meet a man whom I instantly took a liking to. There was a hint of laughter in his eyes, as if he knew I was going to be blown away by what he was about to show me.

Andrew, it turns out, is a man with passions and they are in evidence all around him, from the ultra light aircraft parked in the barn, to the barn itself, which is actually designed to accommodate an elephant (he hopes, someday). He has a fine collection of antique cars, trucks, motorcycles, and tractors. There is another plane parked out on the expansive grassy hilltop. Earlier that day he had taken the delivery of a brand new Kenworth dump truck, but that was for the Highways Department for which Andrew is the superintendent.

Why a treehouse? Because Andrew likes to keep things exciting. More than twenty years ago, when the pines were a bit shorter, Andrew planted three telephone poles in the ground and built this treehouse, which he has lived in ever since that day (except when he's in Sri Lanka logging with elephants). One of the most resourceful and mechanically gifted men I've ever met, he's constructed an elevator to hoist himself up to his forty-two-foot-high abode. Controlled by a motor with a Volvo transmission on the ground, a crane arm above drops a cable to a two-person cage. Andrew demonstrated this extraordinary creation, then invited me into the cage and we made a rotating ascent to the platform above. It was hard to believe it had been built twenty years before; Andrew takes great care of his minimalist home. I've never seen a man live so simply, but he has all the basics: a shower, sink, hot plate, refrigerator, reading chair, and writing desk made of hemlock. Up a small ladder, the attic is his bedroom. Fifty feet off the ground, on top of a hill, Andrew Thurnheer dreams of perching atop elephants in Sri Lanka.

Above: Thurnheer controls his ascents and descents with a handheld remote. Before he built this elevator, he climbed a telephone pole to reach his abode.
Opposite: Like a birdhouse balanced in a high branch, this treehouse looks right at home in the forest.

UPPERMOST TREEHOUSE

Portland, Maine, USA

Peter Lewis's treehouse is so interesting that one could write an entire book about it. He did, actually. It's entitled *Treehouse Chronicles: One Man's Dream of a Life Aloft* published in 2005. Peter was kind enough to send me a copy in Spain so that I could review it and write a blurb for the dust jacket. That was a first, and I was happy to write how Peter had captured something that we need to be reminded of everyday: It's the journey, not the destination. In his book Peter deftly moves between the demands of a young family, a full-time job as a publisher, and an all-consuming construction project in his backyard. It took two years, but his treehouse dream came true. Along the way, through introspective and often hilarious writing (and some great pictures and watercolors), the reader gains a new friend.

I wanted to meet this guy I had become friends with over time and distance in person. So when I was visiting my parents in Portland, Maine, I grabbed my dad and my camera and headed an hour north to check in with Peter.

Right: The Dr. Seuss staircase actually raises and folds in on itself with the push of a button. **Opposite:** Uppermost Treehouse is a two-hundred-and-fifty-square-foot labor of love. It is documented in a beautiful book, *Treehouse Chronicles: One Man's Dream of a Life Aloft,* by the builder, Peter Lewis.

Only by reading his book can one get an inkling of the amount of brainpower that went into this treehouse. Everything was meticulously planned and lovingly executed. I marveled at Peter's Rube Goldberg–like contraptions: stairs that magically rise up by pulling a secret handle near the base of the tree; or a front door lock that would make an Amish carpenter weep. His building partner and erstwhile mentor, Ted Walsh, crafted a chess set so delightful it seems the treehouse was built around it. There is even a handmade water clock that measures time in forty-one-minute units, or "the length of time it takes to carefully read aloud Paul Gallico's classic story, 'The Snow Goose' (actual reading time is several minutes less, but extra time is built in for wiping away tears)." Photographs of these inventions do not do them justice.

Peter calls his treehouse an office, but it's really just a place where he can go to be by himself—very different from being alone, he carefully points out. "If someone climbs quietly up to the treehouse and peeks at me through the window while I'm working, they may think I'm merely taking a nap. This is part of the work of solitude, part of being with me. Thinking, considering, observing, pondering—these are the tools of my trade and occasionally they have to be wielded lying down with my cap pulled down over my eyes." Peter is a modern day Thoreau, only his Walden Pond happens to be an eastern white pine.

Right: The cold Maine winters necessitate a small woodstove, seen at right. **Opposite:** An intricate weave of branches creates a whimsical railing and delicate chair. It extends to support a highly unique chess board. **Overleaf:** Every detail of Peter's treehouse was meticulously planned and lovingly executed. He devised an ingenious sling system that enabled the treehouse to basically hang by cables from a crotch higher in the tree. No significant penetrations were therefore needed in the tree. Other ingenious contraptions abound, such as the hanging rock pile in the center of the picture, which serves as a counterbalance for the retractable stairway.

AMELIA'S TREEHOUSE
Surrey, England

Designer James Hatt built this gem of a treehouse in England. Hatt collaborated with a photographer and stylist to create what they call the "treehouse equivalent of a patchwork quilt" for a photo shoot. Built in just three days with a small team of carpenters "using salvaged doors and windows and any recycled industrial materials we could find," there is something pleasing and timeless about it. When I saw it I knew I had to feature it in this book. The details and organic qualities are superb. After the photo shoot, the treehouse was left in place as a gift for the grandchildren of the property owner.

Right: In a young forest this treehouse pivots around a tree, creating two unique rooms. **Opposite:** The recycled building materials, though not weatherproof, should inspire any aspiring treehouse builder: An unwritten tenet of treehouse building states that one must use as much reclaimed material as possible.

FINCA BELLAVISTA

Costa Rica

Matt and Erica Hogan were traveling in Costa Rica when a dream popped into their heads: They had just taken a tour of an inspiring piece of property on Costa Rica's Southern Pacific coast one fateful day when Erica wondered aloud if a treehouse wouldn't be the perfect structure for a property like that. And then she wondered if people would be interested in living in treehouses within a community, like the Ewok village in *Return of the Jedi*. The idea struck a chord and now the world has its first planned treehouse eco-development.

Their three hundred acres of beautiful secondary forest has it all: big trees, gurgling streams, cascading waterfalls, and all the telltale noises of the jungle. Treehouse designer Roderick Romero was the first to take on a job at what is now called Finca Bellavista. They picked a prime location on which to build the first treehouse—just above a twenty-foot waterfall but far from the hustle and bustle of everyday living—which is being used as a model for potential buyers to view and stay in for a short period of time to get a feel for what it's like to live in a treehouse.

Matt and Erica sold out the thirty-lot first phase of the seventy-two-lot development quickly. A new phase is currently on the drawing boards, but in the meantime a sustainable infrastructure is being established. There is a hydroelectric power plant using water from the namesake Rio Bellavista that runs through the property, solar power, a recycling center, and a common garden area. There is even high-speed Internet via satellite and a WiFi zone. Eventually, there will be zip lines and cable systems to help navigate the hilly and rocky terrain. Otherwise, transportation is strictly by foot, as no cars will be allowed within certain boundaries.

"We wanted to bring something totally different and adventurous into people's lives," Matt says. I'm thinking of establishing a "pied-a-tree" there myself.

Above: For this tropical treehouse two platforms were constructed high in the tree, one ten feet above the other.
Right: Cocktail hour is enhanced by a beautiful waterfall in the distance.
Opposite: Roderick's skill in designing a treehouse in harmony with its environment is unmatched. This treehouse was but a few months old when these photographs were taken, yet it looks as if it has lived happily in these trees for decades.

BRAZIL

Every spring our company receives a handful of e-mails from students looking for internships during the summer. One intern we had—Chris Yorke of Topeka, Kansas—made out particularly well through this experience because at the end of his internship he walked away from Treehouse Point with an all-expenses-paid trip around the world. The deal was this: Chris would take photographs of treehouses in other countries for me since I wouldn't have the time to travel the globe. The problem that an organized soul like Chris faced, however, was that we were rarely sure the treehouses we had earmarked actually existed. It was often stressful and always hard work, but he did a marvelous job. His first stop was Brazil.

THE LAKE HOUSE
Araras, São Paulo

Our lucky intern arrived in Sao Paulo where he met Ricardo Brunelli, owner of Casa na Arvore, Brazil's preeminent treehouse building company. Ricardo immediately whisked him off on a four-treehouse, seven-day tour.

As Chris would soon discover, Ricardo is adept at attracting well-heeled clients. This first example is near the town of Araras and is located on a stunning lake, which is on the grounds of an enormous estate. The treehouse is used as a luxurious retreat for relaxation and entertaining guests.

Below: Clearly built for the enjoyment of the entire family, this spectacular structure spans an entire grove of eucalyptus trees. **Opposite:** Rising three levels, the treehouse provides ample shade for activities on the beach below. **Overleaf, left:** An immense centerpiece with subtle hues and smooth bark, a eucalyptus tree dominates the main room. **Overleaf, right:** Elegant teak and mahogany woodwork delights visitors to this treehouse. Ricardo invites ideas and collaborations with many artists when planning his treehouses.

Right: Ricardo Brunelli's designs are expertly executed by José Aparecido Rossato and his sons. Here, he takes advantage of the lower section of a long knee brace to create a stair landing and transitional walkway that leads to a stairway and the main level above. **Below:** I'm not sure I could get Charlie Greenwood to sign off on bracing like this, but it's beautiful and it looks like it is doing a decent enough job. **Opposite, above:** A comfortable dining area is tucked between trees in the back on the main floor. **Opposite, below:** A playroom for the kids is set off to the edge of the main deck. The playhouse has bunk beds inside, a slide and a climbing wall outside, and even a basket to raise and lower from the window.

THE WATERFALL HOUSE

São Manuel

Though Ricardo went to college in New Jersey (he speaks perfect English), his interest in treehouses grew quite independently of the attention they received in America and other parts of the world. Ricardo designs his treehouses and Jose Aparecido Rossato & Sons, fifth-generation woodworkers, build the structures.

This second example of Ricardo's work was outside the town of São Manuel on the land of a wealthy cattle rancher. An elaborate sequence of swimming pools and waterfalls leads to a bridge that brings visitors to a host of mango trees. A simple but well-appointed cabin awaits you at the top of the stairs. Three separate outdoor decks wrap around this treehouse, and the interior consists of a living room, bathroom, and bedroom. It has everything one needs to relax and enjoy life.

Right: In this treehouse, Ricardo incorporates creative woodworking and inset lighting. Trunks through the decking happily disrupt all the straight lines.
Opposite: Thirty feet in the air, this cozy treehouse hides behind a jumble of railings and mango leaves. It is called the Waterfall House because you pass a number of beautiful water features on the way to this arboreal retreat.

Opposite, above: The approach to the treehouse requires traversing a crow's nest encompassing a mango tree.
Opposite, below: Elevated walkways spider beneath the main platform. Ricardo's creations tend to be placed high in his host trees and he takes full advantage of the space below deck to transport the visitor upwards. **Left:** Traveling the world solo leads one to, occasionally, talk to birds. At least photographer Chris Yorke was able to get some answers, albeit rote, from this guy.
Below: At the highest level, adjacent to the living room, a large deck beckons.

SANTO ANTONIO TREEHOUSE
Santo Antonio da Platina

Below: Under this crazy grove of Jacaranda trees the ground slopes away, allowing a twenty-foot-high deck on the downhill side. **Right, above:** With a view like this and a deck three times the size of the house itself, inevitably guests will spend most of their time outdoors. **Right, below:** Oversize doors, large eaves, and a fold-down outdoor table make this treehouse a perfect summertime retreat.

A wealthy rancher had Ricardo build this simple one-room treehouse in a dense grove of beautiful native Jacaranda trees. Twice a year the trees blossom with beautiful purple flowers. There is a wood stove and a bed in the treehouse, but for the bathroom you have to take a short walk uphill to the main house.

PORECATU TREEHOUSE

Porecatu

About three hundred miles west of São Paulo in a rural area called Porecatu, a classic treehouse beckons visitors into its leafy realm. A mature beech-like Rauli tree is the perfect host as it rises above the surrounding forest to provide incredible views of the awesome Paranapanema River basin. Ricardo and his carpenter family crew could not have done a better job of fitting this fully appointed house into the tree. It is used as a weekend residence by a large, extended family.

Below: This treehouse is a true rainforest retreat. **Opposite:** Thirty feet up a gentle giant of a tree, this treehouse sports balconies and decks offering stunning views into the canopy and surrounding countryside. **Overleaf:** A kitchenette, wood stove, and full bathroom give this treehouse all the comforts of home.

Right: Beneath the treehouse, integrated into the knee braces, a catwalk skirts the tree. **Below:** If the upper deck isn't high enough for visitors they may choose to climb even higher into the tree itself. **Opposite, above and below:** A commanding position at the edge of a forest draws visitors to the sky deck to take in the inspiring views of the Paranapanema River basin.

DARNA SCHOOL TREEHOUSE

Tangier, Morocco

Sean Gillett befriended Roderick Romero (page 62) while volunteering at El Jardin Del Paraiso, a tiny community garden in New York City where Roderick had built a small treehouse several years ago. When Sean's girlfriend at the time, Yto Barrada (they are now married with a child), was visiting New York from Tangier, an idea was hatched that turned into a small miracle. Yto spoke of Darna, an organization in Tangier that takes impoverished children, ages twelve to sixteen—some right off the streets—and teaches them carpentry. Yto said, "What if you two came to Tangier and built a treehouse with these kids?"

Within weeks Sean, who knew how to establish a non profit, and Roderick, who knew how to raise funds, were in business as the 212 Society, a United States sister organization to the non profit in Tangier. It happened to be the year I was in Spain, so when word came that Daryl and Bubba were going to be right across the Strait of Gibraltar, I hopped on a plane and joined them for the last few days of the project.

What I witnessed was utterly heartwarming. These kids in their royal-blue smocks were enthralled by the task of building a treehouse—it was written all over their faces. The treehouse is in the shape of a boat, symbolizing the kids' hope for the future and a better life. Roderick and Sean did a beautiful thing.

Below: Sean Gillett sits while compiling a work-team list as Darna's saint-like teacher, Jaber Bouhout, explains the game plan for the day.

Left: A giant fichus tree reaches its branches out toward the second-story sun deck of an adjacent house. The young carpentry students decided to take advantage of this natural support for a bridge.

Below: The boat-like shape of the platform is pointed directly across the Strait of Gibraltar, which is visible from almost anywhere on the property. Many of these young men yearn to travel across the strait to make a better life for themselves in Europe.

INDIA

Chris Yorke arrived in Mumbai, India, at the beginning of March 2008 only to embark on the second leg of his arduous journey to the famous Green Magic treehouses in the south. To get there he caught a flight to Calicut, then took a two-hour taxi ride through the state of Kerala, and finally a one-hour Jeep Rodeo that landed him in a magical place indeed.

GREEN MAGIC TREEHOUSE
Wayanad

As Chris arrived at Green Magic, an Indian couple from Sunnyvale, California, was descending from the ninety-foot-high treehouse in a water-counterbalanced elevator. It takes two able-bodied helpers to operate the lift, so within moments of his arrival Chris took advantage of the operators' availability and was whisked high into the arboreal abode. (He later discovered that the operators were not always available but luckily were within earshot, but that is another story.)

The Green Magic has two queen-size beds and one bathroom. The owners are in the middle of building a second treehouse, but in the meantime the existing treehouse serves one couple or a close-knit group. The food here is a step up from the local fare and is served on banana leaf plates—a sure sign that one is living in a jungle.

Above: Woven palm fronds and skilled rope work soften the roof structure that works hard to shed rain for several months of the year—usually June through September. **Right:** A metal spiral staircase arrives at the second level, which houses a queen sized bed and sitting area. **Opposite:** It is a commitment to seek out this treehouse, which is in a remote location, but once you arrive it is easy to see how Green Magic got its name.

Opposite: The water-counterbalanced lift takes guests up ninety feet to the treehouse, where there is a queen-size bed and a full-size bath for a long and refreshing soak; a metal spiral staircase leads up to a second bed and a sitting area. It is wonderful to see the vast array of creative interpretations of space in the free-form world of treehouses.
Above: In India, the monsoon season requires a watertight roof, but the walls remain wide open. Mats are on the floor to take the edge off the cold steel that makes up the main floor of the house. Apart from the steel of the superstructure, bamboo is the primary building material.

EDAKKAL HERMITAGE TREEHOUSE
Wayanad

Within striking distance of the Green Magic Treehouse, is a small
treehouse hermitage in the town of Edakkal overlooking a beautiful valley.
As usual, the trip entailed more than the jeep driver originally revealed,
but in the end there is the reward of a perfect example of a quintessential,
simple treehouse.

Below: The popularity of the Green
Magic Treehouse rubbed off on a neighboring town. This is another, far simpler
treehouse that is also available for
overnight stays. **Opposite:** The treehouse
sits atop a knoll, so the views stretch out
forever. It is made primarily of bamboo.

SAFARI LAND RESORT TREEHOUSES

Bokkapuram, Masinagudi

Below: Bamboo, while a strong and plentiful building material, does not do well if it stays wet. In fact, it deteriorates rather quickly so it is important to seal it and to keep it away from areas where moisture is an issue. For that reason, most of the structural posts and the floor joists in this treehouse are made of indigenous sapling hardwood trees. While the treehouse may look rickety, strong and skillfully lashed manila ropes make it sturdy. **Opposite:** The treehouses here are quite substantial, each with its own small bath and dining areas. The food in all of these resort establishments is prepared by chefs and brought into the trees.

This is where you want to go if you wish to see elephants scratching their backs on the trees below you. There are four good-size treehouses to stay in, and the promise of several more once the renovation of the neighboring property (formerly the Wild Canopy Reserve Hotel) is complete. But be prepared! Elephants are not to be treated lightly. At one point, over the din caused by a herd of the brush-rustling pachyderms, Chris noticed his guide, Goutam, rolling up the legs of his pants in preparation for a mad dash to safety. It was more excitement than our mild-mannered photographer had bargained for, but he nonetheless managed to squeeze off a few shots of the soon-to-be-renovated treehouses before hightailing it to safety.

Opposite: In India, bamboo is the predominant natural building material, which gives these treehouses a tropical appearance. **Left:** Plenty of posts keep this house in the tree, but I can't help but wonder if the tree itself is being stressed by the stone bulk works at its base. Arborists insist that root compaction is one of the worst things for the health of a tree. **Below:** It is said that our blood pressure drops when we ascend into the trees, perhaps because we feel safer, less vulnerable, in trees.

THAILAND

DOI KHAM PHRUEKSA RESORT
Chiang Mai

It's hard work, but someone's gotta do it: Following a tenuous treehouse lead, Chris Yorke endured a fourteen-hour train ride from Bangkok to the northern Thai city of Chiang Mai, which brought him to the doorstep of a tiny hotel miles outside of the city. There, a beautiful treehouse awaited him, and he was able to rest tranquilly for two days. "It's a little playpen," he said. He encountered a little green frog in the toilet that sits in a separate small room halfway down the stairway, which when you live in a tree is an indication that all is well.

Right: A fan above the writing desk helps keep the warm and humid air from overcoming occupants. **Below:** There is something magical about having a tree run through the center of a treehouse. The only problem is that it is nearly impossible to keep the roof from leaking, which can become a maintenance nightmare. **Opposite:** With a tree like this in the backyard, how could you *not* build a treehouse?

Above: I'm not sure if this grass gasket
is for insulation purposes or is meant
to prevent bug traffic, but it is easy
on the tree and it looks good to boot.
Opposite: This one room hotel has a
strict "shoes off" policy. They provide
slippers, but they proved to be of
no use to Chris who stands 6 feet 6
inches tall and wears size 13 shoes.
Overleaf: A friendly house appears to
have crash landed in a perfect tree.

PAI TREEHOUSE

Pai, Maehongson

Further south in Thailand, Chris's next stop was at the Pai Treehouse. Getting there was another challenge, but when he finally arrived at the guest house it was a paradise. This is where people can be found casually riding by on elephants!

Right: A crazy set of stairs leads up to a mysterious treetop fantasy world.
Opposite: Somehow this treehouse reminds me of my favorite childhood book called *Go Dog Go!* in which dogs travel from far and wide to attend a party held up in a tree.

Right: Pink Disneyland sleeping bags await you in the uppermost of three separate treehouses. **Below:** Pai is about as remote as one can get, but the farther one goes off the beaten path, the better the rewards can be. That maxim definitely applies to this place. **Opposite:** The more treehouses I see around the world, the more it becomes clear how similar humans are, no matter where you live. For example, we all tend to use materials that are readily available locally and craft them into treetop dwellings that bring us closer to nature and to that feeling of joy that only a treehouse perched among trees can bring. That particular joy is universal.

KHAO SOK TREEHOUSE RESORT

Khao Sok

After a four-hour bus ride from Krabi on the southwest coast of Thailand, Chris Yorke met up with a kind-hearted hotelier named Sakda Samwong, who had set up shop on the edge of the Khao Sok National Park. Mr. Samwong's hotel consists of five hybrid treehouses, which are only partially supported by the trees, with a communal kitchen and dining room. When Chris arrived, all the rooms were occupied, so he had to find lodging elsewhere, but he managed to snap a few photos before the light faded.

Right: Red lacquered posts and glowing lanterns lead up to a house that relies mostly on posts for support. It is also attached to one large tree in the back that is doing its fair share of the work. **Opposite:** This treehouse is still under construction, but it will soon provide sanctuary for guests. **Overleaf:** More and more treehouse hotels are popping up around the world. This complex of hybrid treehouses at the Khao Sok Treehouse Resort have become popular with tourists and, obviously, I think that is a wonderful thing.

THE KULKUL TREEHOUSES

Ubud, Bali, Indonesia

The Ubud area on the island of Bali has yielded three remarkable tree-houses, each of which houses a pair of wooden bells called *kulkuls*. These "signal logs" were once used to warn the local community of imminent danger. Now the deep and resonant sounds the logs make when struck ceremoniously call the community together for important business, such as weddings and funerals.

The treehouse below is just off the main street in downtown Ubud, a thriving arts community and tourist destination located far inland. The tree-house is perched about fifteen feet up in an enormous suar tree. The growth of the tree is rather handily deconstructing the intricately carved stone stairway at its base, but it is a stunning tree nonetheless and, like so many of the mature trees on the island, a shrine sits at its base with offerings to the tree's resident nature spirits.

Above: This small shrine sits at the base of a tree housing three wooden bells, or *kulkuls*. Striking the kulkuls with particular rhythmic patterns communicates specific messages far and wide. **Right:** The tree functions as a tower (albeit a living one) that holds aloft a house with two kulkuls. **Opposite:** This banyan tree is centrally located halfway between Ubud and the airport. **Overleaf:** The beautiful treehouse in Ubud. The elaborately carved stone stairway spirals toward the treehouse.

THE GLOUCESTER AND BICENTENNIAL TREEHOUSE LOOKOUTS
Pemberton, Australia

Australia needs to get to work on their treehouse stock. No world tour would be complete without checking in with the great Down Under, yet despite Chris Yorke's best efforts, a three-week search yielded little fruit. One fine exception is in western Australia. Years ago I had read of the fire lookouts in Pemberton Forest. The two lookout houses that we discovered are basically small cages set impossibly high in the native karri trees, a type of eucalyptus found only in southwestern Australia. These cages were used as actual fire lookouts into the 1970s. Now they are used just for fun, but because of their height they are not for the faint of heart. The two featured here sit atop the Gloucester tree at two hundred feet and the Bicentennial tree at 246 feet. They are the two highest "treehouses" in the world. I'm not big on heights, so I'm glad to have sent Chris instead. He reported that the climb was exhilarating, but despite the solid anchors in the tree he felt rather exposed.

I find the stairs most interesting, as they are a testimony to the resilience of trees despite humans' best efforts to inflict injury—death by a thousand cuts, as it were. The karri tree, however, perseveres, in part because of its natural density and strength. Sydney streets were once paved with blocks of karri wood.

Above: A rebar ladder peg emerges from the well-healed wound that was created by the previous ladder system. **Right:** The original wooden lookout cabins have been replaced with steel and aluminum versions. Pictured is the Gloucester lookout. **Opposite:** The Bicentennial tree in Warren National Park. This climb is 246 feet up into the air.

JAPAN

In the five years since my last visit to Japan, Kobayashi Takashi, also known as Taka, has been a busy man. The Japanese treehouse builder has taken on folk-hero status as he spreads his message of the transformative power of nature across the country. In 2007 he published his own book, *Treedom: The Road to Freedom*, in which he takes his readers on a personal journey, building three treehouses along the way. It is a story that speaks to many in his urbanized world, and on a night that I was visiting him, a crowd of 380 twenty-somethings emerged from the bustling streets of Osaka to hear him speak.

Taka's message is very simple: Nature has the power to heal. Like me, he wants to educate the next generation about the very real powers of nature. "Embracing nature is the key to an uncertain future," he says. "Do what you can now to help save and preserve it." His words are well received by Japanese youth, and the seeds are planted for a new generation of environmentalists.

MR. KOBAYASHI'S POND TREEHOUSE
Tochigi Prefecture

The Pond Treehouse two hours north of Tokyo is a direct result of Taka's campaigning. In an effort to bring people out of the cities, a local farmers' group set aside a public reserve on the edge of some abandoned rice fields. They commissioned Taka to build a treehouse there in the hopes that young people would come out for a picnic, fall in love with the area, and decide to stay and live in the village and become farmers. It's not yet clear if the plan is working, but the local community got a great treehouse out of the deal.

It rests in the branches of an evergreen oak and overlooks a small irrigation pond and the abandoned rice fields beyond. It's a quiet, peaceful setting, and the treehouse fits harmoniously into the environment.

The first thing I noticed was the beautiful woodcarvings throughout the structure. Arabesque designs are carved into a main post, and the beams have bone patterns carved into their ends. They reminded me of Antoni Gaudi and his famous century-old Casa Batllo in Barcelona.

Above: Every post, beam, and board is given respectful attention. **Opposite:** A distinguishing feature of Taka's treehouses is his use of multiple landings. Ascending to his treehouses is a delightful set of experiences at different levels on the way up.

IWASE FARM TREEHOUSE
Fukushima Prefecture

Japan fascinates me. Last time I was there in 2003 everybody smoked; now they don't. It's as though someone flipped a switch, revealing an inclination toward group-think. That's not to say everyone quit. The farmers up in Fukushima prefecture didn't get that memo, but they did hear about Mr. Kobayashi. They had him build a treehouse at the Iwase Farm in the flat fertile soils north of Tokyo.

Iwase Farm is both a working farm and a tourist destination that mandates education in the hopes of attracting young Japanese into the business of farming. The treehouse, built in 2007, is attracting attention on its own. On the day I was there, every person who came through the farm made a beeline for it.

Right: Taka has a fine eye for balancing the straight line with the curved, and his love of the surf shines through in the carvings shown here. **Opposite:** A comforting space is created using multiple levels.

Right: A carved carousel post holds up the roof rafters. **Opposite:** The beautiful hand carved post balances nicely with the hard lines of the treehouse and softer lines of the host tree.

BEACH ROCK TREEHOUSE
Okinawa

A blend of '70s-style communal living and good old-fashioned capitalism awaited us at Beach Rock Village on the subtropical outpost of Okinawa. Beach Rock is a resort of sorts for the backpacker set and specifically for the younger Japanese generation looking for alternatives. It's a magical place, really, with a staff on this November day far outnumbering the guests. One can trade work for room and board, so by design many creative and wondrous projects are rising out of the lush hillside that overlooks a crashing Pacific Ocean in the distance.

Taka's treehouse is one such creation. High in the boughs of an overgrown Chinese hackberry tree rests a Plexiglas portal to the universe. It was built collaboratively in 2005 and was well documented in Taka's book and DVD *Treedom: The Road to Freedom*. It is the only treehouse I'm aware of that was built expressly for the purpose of communicating with outer space. Whether it works or not I cannot say, but one amazing thing about it is that it can withstand severe weather. A typhoon ripped through in 2006, removing some sizable limbs from the tree, but the remarkable dome remained unscathed.

Above: Welcome to Beach Rock Village. **Right:** The journey upward to the treehouse begins with whimsical stairs and ladders. Organic forms abound in Taka's work. **Opposite:** The limbs of a Chinese hackberry tree, reaching out like tentacles, hold the treehouse aloft.

Right: The treehouse appears quite fragile, yet it can withstand severe weather. **Below:** In contrast to the metal and Plexiglas exterior, the plaster walls inside inspire patience within. **Opposite:** The café affords an incredible view over the valley and along the bluff to the treehouse. A dumbwaiter sits below, waiting to be called into use. Food and drink are sent up top from the kitchen and bar below.

A sparkling beacon among treetops, it is easy to imagine the dome succeeding at its mission to make contact with alien life.

THE DRIFTWOOD EGG TREEHOUSE

Hokkaido

On the extreme opposite end of Japan, on the northern island of Hokkaido, is another fantastic creation by Taka and his merry team of carpenters. This driftwood egg-in-a-tree was created for a Nescafé commercial, in which Taka and a famous Japanese personality sip coffee for the camera looking buzzed and beautiful for a thirty-second spot. Apparently a treehouse, like sex, sells.

Right: The driftwood coiffure gives a cartoonish, almost human quality to this treehouse. **Opposite, above:** Taka used driftwood gathered in Obihiro on the northern island of Hokkaido to construct this tiny treehouse, which hovers twelve feet above the ground and is only nine feet in diameter. It remains in this field, a beautiful landmark but sadly off-limits to curious townspeople. **Opposite, below:** The treehouse seems so fragile humbly nestled into this solitary tree.

LAZY EYES TREEHOUSE
Kawasaki

An hour-long train ride from Tokyo took us to another of Taka's amazing treehouse projects—a small, private oasis owned by an individual who wants to share the beauty of his surroundings with those who appreciate it.

Right, above: A skylight (at left) doubles as a trapdoor. One can climb onto the low-pitch cedar-bark roof and relax out in the open beneath the branches. **Right:** This treehouse features stained glass by artist Jahpon. **Opposite:** The long bridge thrills visitors to this simple one-room treehouse hiding among the leaves.

Above: Stained-glass eyes over the
entrance greet visitors. Inside the
treehouse hangs Taka's signature hammock. A ladder leads up to the roof.
Opposite: The treehouse floats on stilts
and knee braces above a lower deck.

BIG BEACH IN THE SKY TREEHOUSE

Nanshan, Hainan Province, China

Great sand dunes separate Nanshan's treehouses from the blue expanse of the South China Sea. It is a breathtakingly beautiful location that barely hints at the mind-boggling development that is happening just up the coast on China's Hainan Island.

The Nanshan Buddhist Cultural Park, in which this group of four delightful treehouses is located, is a relatively new venture comprised of an enormous temple (supporting more than fifty monks), elaborate gardens, villas to rent (in addition to the four treehouses), and the largest statue of Buddha in Southeast Asia. At 350 feet tall the statue is far larger than the Statue of Liberty and sits on its own man-made island a quarter mile off the sandy beach. It is quite a sight to behold, and you can see it from two of the treehouses.

Ten years ago, American designer David Greenberg conspired to build these treehouses with his Chinese counterparts. He recruited treehouse builder and pioneer Michael Garnier, and together with a team of skilled local carpenters and craftspeople they created a truly magical enclave in the boughs of a mature tamarind forest. The main treehouse, "the big beach in the sky" as Greenberg calls it, can sleep up to six people. It connects by a chain bridge to a small two-person treehouse perched higher on the dunes. A third treehouse sleeps four and provides, on the ground level, a common bathroom with a toilet, shower, and hot and cold running water. The fourth treehouse was built in a traditional Hawaiian hale style and is sited at the entrance to the enclave (this one was featured in my last book).

While the arboreal village definitely has a rustic feel to it, the rest of Nanshan is decidedly upscale, and the hale treehouse now houses the staff. In fact, the treehouses come with a full-time butler, and you can order breakfast, lunch, and dinner without ever leaving your hammock.

Above: The main path to the big tree-house winds directly beneath a low hanging beam. **Below:** Follow the path leading away from Big Beach in the Sky up to the top of the dunes; on the left, overlooking the South China Sea, stands a 350-foot statue of Buddha. **Opposite:** The Big Beach in the Sky has more character than just about any treehouse I have ever visited. It was a particular joy to visit this treehouse not only because I had been hearing about it from Michael Garnier for years, but also because my good friend Taka from Japan agreed to meet me there.

Right: When building a treehouse, it is important to keep in mind that nothing needs to be done precisely the way it would be done in a typical house. For example, there is no need for straight lines: If a branch obstructs the area where a doorway might be, simply shape the door to fit the space (and watch your head). David Greenberg, the creator of this place, takes that notion to new heights in these wonderful treehouses. **Below:** Crafty built-ins like this seat are plentiful. **Opposite:** What is it about a simple winding stair cut to fit a gnarled trunk that appeals to so many people?
Overleaf: In the foreground the bridge connects to an ample deck that lands in the dunes from which guests can head out to the beach. A second sleeping house is elevated above the deck and serves as a roof over an open dining area below. The salt air is taking its toll on the steel-bridge attachments, but the treehouse itself is holding up marvelously well in its old tamarind tree.

CAMBODIA

THE FRIENDSHIP TREEHOUSE
Siem Reap

The goodwill of Mr. Kobayashi, a.k.a. Taka, spread to Cambodia in the spring of 2007. As part of a cultural alliance, Japan has been funding much of the restoration costs for the famous Angkor Wat temples near the growing city of Siem Reap. The Japanese government also managed to earmark some funds to sponsor a treehouse on the grounds of the historical landmark, and Taka was handed the job.

When I found out that my friend was returning to Cambodia to deliver some additional funds to help finish the project, I thought it would be a good idea to join him. After all, it was January and raining in Seattle, and the temples at Angkor Wat have always been high on my list of places to visit.

The treehouse winds its way eighty feet up a gargantuan "chitiel" tree, which I was told, grows only in that area of the world. Taka climbed seven of them before choosing the one in which he would build. It was the only one from which he could catch a glimpse of the tallest towers of Angkor Wat's temples. The treehouse is made up of six separate platforms each with a sturdy ladder connecting it to the next. Climbing to the top is in no way a comfortable experience—there are no railings—but this is precisely why Taka had returned to remedy this situation. Through his own private fundraising efforts back in Japan he managed to raise $3,000 to pay for the installation of the new railings. Both countries can now breathe a collective sigh of relief.

Above: You can watch the sun set directly over the towers of the famous temples of Angkor Wat from this little observation hut. **Below:** Despite the lack of railings, the eighty-foot climb up the ladder to the treehouse has been practiced repeatedly by those in the know. There are no signs directing the public to the location of this treehouse, but judging by the number of signatures on the interior walls, many have braved the ascent. **Opposite:** The scalloped red roof is in keeping with vernacular architecture, but that is where the similarities end. The siding, for instance, is pure Taka.

FISHERMEN'S STILT HOUSE AND TREEHOUSE SHRINE

Kompong Phhluk

One of the great side trips in my treehouse adventure in Asia was a visit to the fishing village of Kompong Phhluk. Halfway through a difficult taxi ride from Siem Reap, Taka and I were tailed by a few savvy motorbikers. When the taxi could go no further, we jumped on the backs of the motorbikes and were delivered deeper into the delta to an established but transient port. We jumped aboard a narrow version of the *Delta Queen* and bushwhacked our way out to wider water courses until we encountered the strange lives of fishermen in Cambodia. Two or three miles later we arrived in this fishing village on stilts.

Below: What Taka and I found in the flooded forest of Kompong Phhluk was positively other worldly: It was an entire village of stilt houses sitting over water at least fifteen feet into the air. **Opposite:** We discovered one very small shrine close to the mouth of the river that looks like a treehouse to me.

RESOURCES

BUILDERS/CRAFTSPEOPLE/FRIENDS

TreeHouse Workshop Inc.
Consulting, Design, Construction,
Workshops
PO Box 17819
Seattle, WA 98127
206-782-0208
www.treehouseworkshop.com
Pete Nelson
Send me your best treehouse photos!
pete@treehouseworkshop.com

The Global Treehouse Symposium
c/o the Global Treehouse Network
An annual gathering of treehouse
enthusiasts in mid-September in
Fall City, WA
www.globaltreehousenetwork.com

Charles Greenwood
Treehouse engineer
www.treehouseengineering.com

Free Spirit Spheres
Tom Chudleigh
www.freespiritspheres.com

Dan Mac
Furniture builder and wood sculptor
www.danielmack.com

Hugh Lofting
Timber framer and bon vivant
West Grove, PA
www.ghloftingtimberframe.com

Forever Young Treehouses Inc.
Universally Accessible Public
Treehouses
Bill Allen
Burlington, VT
www.treehouses.org

Attie Jonker
azzanarts@me.com or attiejonker@
yahoo.com
www.azzanarts.com

Roderick Romero
Treehouse designer
New York, NY
www.romerostudios.com

Ben Brungraber, Ph.D., P.E.
Engineer/Worrier
Fire Tower Engineered Timber, Inc.
60 Valley St.
Unit #1 The Plant
Providence, RI 02909
401-654-4600
www.ftet.biz

Woody Crenshaw
Makers of fine lighting
Floyd, VA
www.crenshawlighting.com

Michael Garnier
Treehouse pioneer and GL supplier
Oregon
www.treehouses.com

Matt and Erica Hogan
Finca Bellavista, a sustainable
treehouse community
La Florida De Osa, Costa Rica
www.fincabellavista.net

Treehouse Island
Where everybody feels like a kid
again
A treehouse community in
Washington State
www.treehouseisland4u.com

Dan Wright
Treetop builders
Pennsylvania
www.treetopbuilders.net

Sahale Bridge Builders
Cable bridge specialists
Carroll Vogel
Seattle, WA
www.sahale.com

Kobayashi Takashi
Treehouse Creations Co., Ltd.
Japanese treehouse builders
www.treehouse.jp

Scott D. Baker
Tree Solutions Inc.
Valuable knowledge of trees
Consulting arborist
www.treesolutions.net

Urban Forest Innovations Inc.
Philip van Wassenaer, chief
consulting arborist
Risk assessment specialist
pwassenaer1022@rogers.com

Cape Cleare Fishery
Premium quality wild Alaskan
salmon, sustainably harvested
direct from the fishermen
Rick Oltman
www.capecleare.com

Hampus
Treehouse builders in Denmark
www.hampus.dk

Michael Ince
Sculptor and treehouse artist
61A Burnett Lane
Brookhaven, NY 11719
631-286-5870

Dr. Olaf K. Ribeiro, Ph.D.
Plant Pathologist
Ribeiro Tree Evaluations, Inc.
10744 NE Manitou Beach Drive
Bainbridge Island, WA 98110
206-842-1157
www.ribeirotreehealth.com

La Cabane Perchee
Treehouse builders in France
www.la-cabane-perchee.com

Out On a Limb Tree Company
Arborist/tree service and women's
world tree-climbing champion
Kathy Holzer

Seattle, WA
206-938-3779
www.outonalimbseattle.com

Jonathan Fairoaks
Consulting arborist and treehouse
builder
Pennsylvania
www.thelivingtreehouse.com

Salisbury Woodworking, Inc.
Wood floors and timber framing
7671 NE Day Road West
Bainbridge Island, WA 98110
206-842-9500
www.salisburywoodworking.com

Brion Toss Yacht Riggers
313 Jackson Street
Port Townsend, WA 98368
Latitude 48 07' 00" North
Longitude 122 45' 06" West
360-385-1080
www.briontoss.com

Kunstlerische Holzgestaltung
Kulturinsel Einsiedel, Germany
Jurgen Bergmann—builder/genius
www.kulturinsel.de

Barbara Butler
Artist-Builder Inc.
San Francisco, CA
www.barbarabutler.com

BT Big Timberworks, Inc.
Extraordinary builders
P.O. Box 368
One Rabel Lane
Gallatin Gateway, MT 59730
1-800-763-4639
www.bigtimberworks.com

Carlos Cortés Tallér/Studios
Faux Bois specialty work
Studio Cortés
1101 South St. Mary's St.
San Antonio, TX 78210
210-472-3966
www.studiocortes.com

TOOLS AND MATERIALS

Duluth Timber Co.
www.duluthtimber.com

Screw Products
Star drive wood screws—the
ultimate
www.screw-products.com

Tree Equipment Supplier
WesSpur Tree Equipment Inc.
1680 Baker Creek Place
Bellingham, WA 98226
1-800-268-2141
www.wesspur.com

New Tribe
Tree climbing equipment
www.newtribe.com

Pioneer Millworks
Farmington, NY
www.pioneermillworks.com

ConvectAir
Electric home heating solutions
www.convectair.com

Earthwise Inc.
Building Salvage
Seattle, WA
www.earthwise-salvage.com

Second Use
Building materials
Seattle, WA
www.seconduse.com

Diamond Pier
Gig Harbor, WA
www.diamondpier.com

Incinolet
www.incinolet.com

Terramai
Reclaimed woods from
around the world
Mt. Shasta, CA
www.terramai.com

American Arborist Supplies Inc.
882 South Matlack St.
West Chester, PA 19382
www.arborist.com

Craigslist
www.craigslist.org

Lindal Cedar Homes
Great Douglas fir wood
windows
www.lindal.com

ORGANIZATIONS

Make a Wish Foundation
www.wish.org

The Hole in the Wall Gang
No-fee camp for youth, ages
seven to fifteen, with cancer and
serious blood diseases
www.holeinthewallgang.org

Longwood Gardens
Kennett Square, PA
www.longwoodgardens.org

International Society of Arborculture
www.isa-arbor.com

IslandWood
www.islandwood.org

U.S. Green Building Council
www.usgbc.org

Building Materials Reuse Association
(BMRA)
6222 Kentucky Avenue
Pittsburgh, PA 15206
www.buildingreuse.org

Julia Butterfly Hill
www.juliabutterflyhill.wordpress.com/

TREEHOUSE LODGING

Treehouse Point
6922 Preston Fall City Rd. SE
Issaquah, WA 98027
425-441-8087
www.treehousepoint.com

Out 'n' About
A treehouse resort in southern
Oregon
www.treehouses.com

Free Spirit Spheres
Qualicum, British Columbia, Canada
www.freespiritspheres.com

The Big Beach in the Sky
Island of Hainan, China
www.treehousesofhawaii.com

Safari Land Resorts
Bokkapuram, Masinagudi, India
www.safarilandresorts.com

Pia Treehouse
Pai, Maehongson, Thailand
www.paitreehouse.com

Khao Sok Tree House Resort
Thailand
www.khaosok-treehouse.com

Tarzan House
Ariau Jungle Lodge, Brazil

Hotell Hackspett
Single treehouse hotel
Sweden
www.mikaelgenberg.com

Cedar Creek Treehouse
www.cedarcreektreehouse.com

Green Magic Treehouse Resort
www.hotelskerala.com/greenmagic

INDEX

ACKNOWLEDGMENTS

I have so many wonderful people to thank for their help and assistance in making this book happen. First and foremost, I thank my wife Judy, who promises to accompany me on more of my boondoggles as we grow old together. Next I thank the interns, Chris Yorke and David Geisen, who when bored one day suggested I call my editor to get another treehouse book lined up. It was a great idea and I hope you both still think so. I am so thankful that you both stuck with me to the bitter end. Thanks to Kobayashi Takashi for all your help in touring Japan and other far-away places. Your work inspires me. Thanks to all of TreeHouse Workshop Inc.: Jake Jacob, Anna Daeuble, Teri Fox, Daryl McDonald, Bubba Smith, Steve Wray, Dave Whitlock, Ron Myhre, Ian Weedman, Ben Smith, and all those who help us, particularly Josh Barnes, Jason Peaton, Roderick Romero, Bruce Blacker, Tom Salisbury, Jim Burgess, Ian Jones, Scott Baker, Charley Greenwood, Lela Hilton, Russell Coxen, and Michael Garnier. I hope we get to build treehouses together for a long, long time.

I would also like to thank all of the people at Abrams who worked so hard to make this such a lovely book: editor-in-chief Eric Himmel, senior editor Andrea Danese and her assistant Caitlin Kenney, and designer Ellen Nygaard.

PHOTO CREDITS

All photographs were taken by author Pete Nelson, except the following:

David Geisen: pages 26–29
James Hatto: pages 136–137
Matt Hogan: pages 138–139
Chris Yorke: pages 140–157, 160–183, 188–189

This book is dedicated to my daughter Emily: What I try to teach her, she ends up teaching me. Her passion and humor delight me to no end.

Text © 2009 by Pete Nelson
Photographs © 2009 by Pete Nelson, except as noted in the photo credits

Editor: Andrea Danese
Designer: Ellen Nygaard
Production Manager: Alison Gervais

THE **ART OF BOOKS** SINCE 1949

115 West 18th Street
New York, NY 10011
www.abramsbooks.com

ISBN 978-1-4351-5007-2

Manufactured in China
10 9 8 7 6 5 4 3

Page 1: Big Beach in the Sky Treehouse in China.
Pages 2–3: Uppermost Treehouse in the USA.
Pages 4–5, *from left to right:* Safari Land Resort Treehouses in India; Canopy Cathedral in the USA; The Driftwood Egg Treehouse in Japan; Porecatu Treehouse in Brazil; Free Spirit Spheres in Canada; Doi Kham Phrueksa Resort in Thailand; Big Beach in the Sky in China.